Children's Edition

FIRM FOUNDATIONS

Creation to Christ

Book 2

by

Trevor McIlwain

with
Nancy Everson

New Tribes Mission, Sanford, FL 32771-1487

Sixth Printing 2003

Book 2

Lessons 1 – 12

with Review Sheets, Skits and Visuals

Visuals of Posters 5-9

IMPORTANT
NOTE TO TEACHERS:

To effectively use these children's lessons,
READ AND STUDY BOOK 1
before you begin
studying and teaching
the lessons themselves.

SUBSTITUTE TEACHERS:

Please see note on page 72 of Book 1.
If you have time, also read and study
Book 1.

PASTORS AND
SUNDAY SCHOOL SUPERINTENDENTS:

Please see note on page 72 of Book 1.
Even though you may not be the one teaching
this material, please read Book 1, which
explains the teaching rationale
used in the lessons.

lesson

1

Introducing the Bible

OVERVIEW

This lesson is designed to introduce the Bible to your students. Included are some interesting facts and general information about the Bible and how it came to us. The main point of this lesson is to establish the fact that the Bible is the Word of God.

This lesson also presents to the students the general guidelines for the entire study:
— God-centered
— chronological
— foundational.

Joshua
1:8

Psalm
19:119

Isaiah
40:8
55:6-11

Luke
24:27,32,
44

John
1:1,2,17

LESSON PREPARATION

This section is for you, the teacher.

The passages in the Scripture Reference column are for your own study in preparing for this lesson. Since they may contain concepts that run ahead of the lesson, they are not to be taught at this point.

Note: Please read carefully the note to teachers in the front of this book.

LESSON GOALS:

* To present the Bible as God's Word — true, without error, and effective.

THIS LESSON SHOULD HELP THE STUDENTS:

* To understand where the Bible came from.
* To gain confidence in its authority.
* To gain respect for its uniqueness as God's written Word.

PERSPECTIVE FOR THE TEACHER:

Many of us live in a society which was founded on biblical principles. Family structure, law and order, morality, social concerns, and many other basic elements of our culture were established by God and clearly recorded in His Word.

Though some people in our society have never set foot inside the door of a church, they have probably heard about the Bible; they may even own one. Other people may go to church week after week but never open their Bibles. Most people in our culture are not unaware of the Bible; but sadly, many do not know what it says because they have never taken the time to read and study it for themselves.

A child's initial view of the Bible is usually based upon how God's Word is treated in his home. But even if the Bible has not been taught at home, children are wonderfully teachable and are eager to learn whatever you present. Since the Word is able to penetrate the minds of skeptical adults, how much more will it touch the hearts of children! As teachers we have before us the wonderful privilege of presenting to the children the Book of books, written by the Lord of lords, the tender, loving heavenly Father and Saviour of the world. This is our opportunity to introduce to them the One God and the one Book that can transform their lives for all eternity.

Pray that God will open the minds and hearts of your students to learn and to believe God's true and living Word, the Bible. [1]

REFERENCE MATERIAL:

Following is a list of books which may help you in preparing for this lesson:

From God to Us—How We Got Our Bible, by Norman L. Geisler and William E. Nix. Moody Press, Chicago, 1974.

What You Should Know About Inerrancy, by Charles C. Ryrie. Moody Press, Chicago, 1981.

Evidence that Demands a Verdict, by Josh McDowell. Here's Life Publishers, San Bernadino, 1979.

You may find additional reference materials such as these a great help in encouraging interested students. Children can ask amazing questions. Don't be

MEMORY
VERSE
II Timothy 3:16

[1] You will probably learn quite a bit about your students' knowledge of the Bible as you go through this lesson. Some of the children may come from homes where the Bible is being taught on a regular basis. But other children may never have held a Bible in their hands.

Be very careful to help the children to find chapters and verses. If your class is large, enlist helpers to assist the children. It is extremely important that each child be able to see in his Bible what is being taught.

Consider even the most elementary question important. If a question is off the subject, you may have to tell a child that you must wait until a later lesson to fully answer. But let him know that you appreciate his interest. If it is appropriate, take time after class to answer his question.

Take every opportunity to encourage your students! ❏

afraid to say, I don't know the answer to your question, but I will try to find the answer for you. You may have to limit the discussion during class time, but be ready to offer additional information to an interested student.

NOTES REGARDING THE INERRANCY OF SCRIPTURE:

The inerrancy of the Scriptures is an extremely important fact. It can be shown to be true through many avenues of proof, some of which are explored more fully in the resource materials listed on the previous page.

For us who teach, it is **vital** that we believe in the inerrancy of the Bible. If you are not clear on this issue yourself, it would be wise to study some of these resources so that your faith can rest more firmly in God's true Word.

But for your students, some of whom may not even be believers, it is **not** essential that you prove or force the issue of inerrancy at this point.

The Bible itself is its own strongest proof. As stated in Hebrews 4:12, *"...the word of God is quick, and powerful, and sharper than any twoedged sword...."*

Children are usually very open and teachable. But you may find that someone has already taught them to doubt God's Word. We need to communicate the facts in such a way that the children are really hearing God's truth. Trust God to apply His Word to their hearts.

VISUALS:

- Chronological Picture No. 1, God's Word Written
- Visual, Timeline
- Visual, Firm Foundations
- Visual, God's Word Through Israel to the World
- Map or globe of the world; map of the Mideast and Israel

The maps could be from a current atlas so that the students may see that you are relating to present-day locations. (In future lessons you will use the Chronological Maps provided with these lessons. Chronological Map 1 may be used for this lesson if you do not have other maps available.)

- If possible, bring to class a few Bibles translated into other languages.
- Poster 1, Learning About God

This poster is in two sections which can be taped together or placed side by side on a bulletin board. You will use this poster for every lesson, so display it in a prominent location. If you are using a bulletin board, you may cover all the attributes of God with separate strips of colored paper and reveal each one when it is first introduced. (On each piece of colored paper mark in small penciled letters which attribute is underneath.) In this lesson, only one attribute is stressed, God communicates with man. You will be showing it on the poster as you cover outline point F. (Other attributes of God are alluded to in this lesson, but will be introduced in later lessons as they are brought out through the Scriptures being taught.)

SPECIAL PREPARATION:

- Make copies for your class of the **Lesson 1 Review Sheet** and **Skit 1** (at the end of this lesson). Provide pencils for the children.
- Photocopy **visuals** (at end of lesson) — use as small posters or for overhead transparencies.
- Prepare for any activity you select from the **Suggestions for Activities** (at the end of this lesson). As you select activities, remember to allow sufficient time to teach the outlined lesson material.

LOOKING AHEAD:

Suggestion: Read through Lesson 4, "God Created the Heavens and the Earth," and consider which reference materials you may want to locate or order and study.

Lesson 1: Introducing the Bible

ON TEACHING THIS LESSON:

You are carefully laying a scriptural foundation on which the Gospel will later be presented. Each lesson builds on previous lessons, so be sure to cover each point carefully.

DON'T COMPLICATE THE MESSAGE!

As you teach, keep in mind that this is a directed study — not an exhaustive survey of the Bible. Keep your lesson on track and moving ahead by limiting and directing any discussion.

Carefully follow the outline. Emphasize the doctrinal themes.

LESSON FORMAT: The **center column** below contains the lesson material to be taught to the students. The **bold outline headings** are only for reference and need not be spoken, as they are incorporated into the outlined material that follows. The material in the **side columns** is for the teacher's own reference and is not intended to be included in the lesson.

TO BE TAUGHT TO THE STUDENTS
(Center Column Only)

LESSON OUTLINE:

PERFORM Skit 1. Note: Uncle Don's part should be read by an adult.

A. Introduction

We are going to study the most wonderful book in the whole world — the Bible! **2**

Does everyone here have a Bible? Hold up your Bible so I can see it.

Did you know that the Bible in your hand is like a personal letter sent to you from God?

Imagine! God has written this book to each one of us so that we can know Him personally!

(You may put your Bibles down now.)

2 Before you begin, make sure that every child has a Bible. ❏

B. God is the focus of our study.*

That's why God gave us the Bible — **He wants us to know Him!**

— God is the central character of the Bible.

— As we study, you will learn what He is really like:

Who He is

What He does

What He is like — His personality.

* Remember that these lettered, bold outline headings are not to be spoken; the thought is included in the lesson text. ❏

C. We will study the Bible chronologically.

The Bible is also the true story of history as seen from God's viewpoint.

We are going to study the Bible in the order in which things really took place.

— Do you know what was there before the beginning? **3**

— Do you know where angels came from?

— Where is God right now?

3 Do not discuss answers to these questions, but do give the children opportunity to think and to express themselves briefly. If they try to answer, agree with them if they are right, but don't correct them if they are wrong. Just tell them that we can only guess, but God has the true answers in the Bible. ❏

In the Bible, God tells us the answers to these and many other questions!

Suggested Visual:

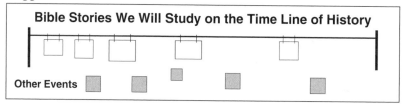

— Explain:

> *A time line shows things in the order in which they happened. We will be stretching out the Bible time line and putting each story we study into its place on that line.*
>
> *Studying this way is a little like stretching out a clothesline and then hanging clothes on it.*
>
> *You may already know about certain details of the Bible but not yet have a clear understanding of where they fit into the overall picture.*
>
> *Maybe you have heard about Abraham and Moses and David. But who came first? Was it Moses or was it Abraham? [Abraham]*
>
> *As we study, you will see how these people and many others fit into history, and you will also see where other things fit in between the things we study.*
>
> *We won't study every story along the line, but we will choose certain stories or events in history that will make all the rest seem to fall into place.* [4]

We are going to begin our next lesson in Genesis, which is where God's story of history begins.

The book of Genesis is the **foundation** of the Bible.

D. We will be laying firm foundations for understanding the Bible.

— Explain:

> *How many of you have seen a house being built?*
>
> *Do the builders start with the roof?*
>
> *No! First they lay the foundation.*
>
>> *The foundation is the very bottom part, usually made of cement or stone.*
>>
>> *It must be very firm and strong so it can hold the weight of the whole building.*
>
> *Then the house is built on top of a firm foundation, one piece at a time.*

Suggested Visual:

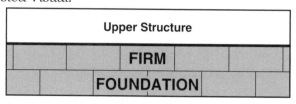

[4] If you have older students in your class who tend to sidetrack the discussion, you may find it helpful to make small posters of the "clothesline" and "foundations" visuals. Then, whenever a student is getting off track from the lesson, you can point to the visual and gently remind him that you are going to cover just the main events and stick to the foundational issues.

Be very careful to acknowledge a student's interest and to encourage him to continue to ask questions. If at all possible, try to give an interested student all the help you can to encourage him to study the Bible on his own. Try to answer his questions after class if it is not appropriate to do so during class time. ❏

If the foundations aren't first built properly, the rest of the house cannot be strong.

For this reason, it is very important that you attend every lesson.

— Everything we study will be important and will become part of the foundation for our future studies.

— If you miss a class, you will find it more difficult to understand later lessons.

So try not to miss any classes! We want to learn together.

E. A look at the Bible

Now let's open our Bibles. [5]

We are going to be using our Bibles every time we meet, so let's begin to learn how to use them.

— Table of Contents

— Old Testament

— New Testament

— Chapters, verse numbers

— Footnotes, various helps.

The Bible is God's Word.

— When we talk about the Bible being God's Word, we are talking about the text of the Bible, not the various notes that men have added. [6]

The Bible means a lot to me.

— Example:

"The Bible is my favorite book. I know that when I read God's Word, I'll find the help I need for every day. The Bible tells me what God is like. He's wonderful! The more I read, the more I want to read and to know Him better." [7]

F. The Bible is the most important book in the whole world because it is the Word of GOD.

 Theme: God is greater than all and more important than all; He is the highest authority.

 Theme: God communicates with man.

READ II Timothy 3:16: **"All scripture is given by inspiration of God...."** [8]

God spoke to men called prophets the exact messages He wanted written down.

— Sometimes He spoke out loud.

— Sometimes He spoke to them in visions.

— Sometimes He just put the message directly into their minds.

— God caused the prophets to write exactly what He spoke to them.

 READ II Peter 1:20,21.

The Bible is not men's ideas, but **God's own Word**.

Teacher's Notes (margin):

[5] Take whatever time is needed to help each child find these things. ❏

[6] Some Bibles have extensive footnotes which can be very misleading. If you are providing Bibles for your students, use Bibles which have only the Bible text without commentary.

If your students have brought their own Bibles, take the time to point out for them, in their Bibles, which part is God's Word and which part is not. ❏

[7] This is not a salvation testimony; rather, it is a simple testimony of your appreciation of the Bible. ❏

[8] Remember that when the verse is printed in the lesson like this, the highlighted portion is the part you want to talk about.

The other part of the verse contains themes that you do not want to cover at this point. Stick to the subject!

Help your students to find this verse, and every passage that will be read. This will take time, but will be well worth the effort. A helper can do this for you — larger classes may need several helpers. ❏

God gave His words to men.

We will begin our "LEARNING ABOUT GOD" poster with this: "God communicates with man."

God communicates with us; that is, He tells us what we need to know!

ON THE POSTER "LEARNING ABOUT GOD" POINT TO "GOD COMMUNICATES WITH MAN." **9**

Suggested Visual:

This picture shows a prophet writing down the message given him by God. The prophet is writing on a scroll, a roll of parchment or leather on which text was written in ink. In those days, scrolls were used instead of paper. The scroll could be rolled up and stored, just like we keep a book on the shelf.

CHRONOLOGICAL PICTURE NO 1, "GOD'S WORD WRITTEN"

No other book in the world was written this way — with God telling men exactly what to write.

God is the author of the Bible.

God used more than 40 men to write down His Words.

The Bible was not written all at once — it took 1,600 years for all of the Bible to be written down!

 Theme: God never changes.

But the Bible reads like one book from beginning to end, because **God is its one Author**.

> *The Bible fits together as one Book, even though God used over 40 men and took over 1,600 years to write it.*

> *God never changes, and He just kept on telling men what to write until everything He wanted to tell us was written down.*

— The only answer for the unity of the Bible is **one author — God!**

G. The Bible is God's message to the world, which He gave through the Jewish people.

 Theme: God communicates with man.

 Theme: God is greater than all and more important than all; He is the highest authority.

All but one of the men whom God used to write His Word were Jewish. (Luke was apparently a Gentile — a Gentile is anyone who is not Jewish.)

SHOW MAP OF WORLD, MIDEAST, ISRAEL. **10**

God gave His message through the Jewish people, but His message is for the whole world.

9 Have the children say the word "communicate" several times until they are familiar with it. Then ask a couple of children to tell you what the word means. It will take time, but this kind of repetition and asking will help teach new words and establish truths in the children's minds.

Review a new word often until you are satisfied that all the children are understanding what the word means.

Note: In this first lesson, this is the only attribute of God you will be referring to on the visual. You are alluding to other attributes but will wait until other lessons to emphasize them through the Scriptures you will be teaching. ❏

10 On the world map show the children where they live. Then show them the area of the mideast. Point out to them the Mediterranean Sea and Israel. Show them that Israel is at the far righthand end of the Mediterranean Sea.

Then have the children try on their own to find Israel on the map. ❏

Isaiah 43:10

Romans 3:1,2

In Isaiah 45:22 God says, *"Look unto me...all the ends of the earth: for I am God, and there is none else."*

Suggested Visual:

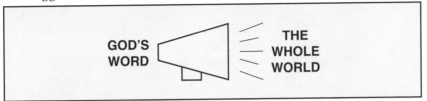

— *Explain:*

You might say that Israel was like God's megaphone or microphone, broadcasting God's message to the whole world.

H. The Bible has been passed down to us intact and with extreme accuracy.

 Theme: God never changes.

[Give each child a copy of the Lesson 1 Review Sheet. As you share the following information, help the children to trace God's Word down the review sheet.]

Originally, God's prophets wrote down God's exact message.

As the original writings wore out from use and age, new copies had to be made.

Copying was done with extreme care.

— The number of letters in a book were counted and the middle letter of a book was given. Also, the number of words were counted and the middle word was marked. [11]

— Though every word was hand copied, there are more ancient copies of the Bible than of any other ancient book.

— All of the very old manuscripts or copies that have been found say the same thing. The only differences are tiny details that do not affect the meaning.

Example:

In 1947, about 15 miles from Jerusalem, a shepherd boy threw a rock into a cave, hoping to scare out one of his animals that had strayed into the cave. He heard the sound of pottery breaking and went inside the cave to investigate. To his amazement, he saw pottery urns holding ancient scrolls. He reported his find, and when scholars investigated, they found hundreds of scrolls. These Dead Sea Scrolls had been hidden in area caves by a religious group sometime during the first century before Christ.

At the time of this discovery, translators were using manuscripts which had been copied around 900 A.D. When scholars compared the Dead Sea Scrolls with the manuscripts which they had been using, there were no meaningful differences! Though separated by 1,000 years, the two copies said the same thing. God preserves His Word.

How did we get the Bible in our language?

— The original books of the Bible were written in either Hebrew, Aramaic, or Greek.

[11] *The Illustrated Bible Dictionary,* Part 3, J. D. Douglas, ed., Inter-Varsity Press, Tyndale House Publishers, Wheaton, IL, 1980. p.1538. ❏

— For many centuries, only a few people were able to have copies of the Bible.

— Down through the ages, God enabled men to translate the Bible into different languages.

> Many copies of the ancient Hebrew, Aramaic, and Greek texts are still in existence.
>
> Translators have studied these as they translated the Bible.
>
> Our Bible truly is the Word of God!

— Today, we have a variety of printed Bibles in our language.

— The Bible has been translated into more languages than any other book. **12**

12 If you have brought Bible translations, show them to the children. ❏

I. The Bible is an accurate historical record.

Does anyone know what an archeologist does?

He is a person who studies the past and digs in the ground to find the things left behind by ancient civilizations.

As archeologists have dug in the area of the lands mentioned in the Bible, they have found many of the things God told us about in His Word.

In fact, many of the places mentioned in the Bible can still be seen today!

The Bible is a true history book, and archeologists have found many pieces of ancient information that agree with what is written in the Bible, even down to the smallest details.

— Exact locations of cities and towns and buildings

— How people lived

— Names

— Dates.

As we study future lessons, we will talk about some of these discoveries.

 Theme: God never changes.

The Bible never needs to be updated or changed.

— When archeologists and students of history make new discoveries, they find that their discoveries agree with what God has already written in the Bible.

— But books written by men, such as school textbooks, encyclopedias, and scientific books, all must be changed every few years as more is learned and old ideas are replaced.

— Example:

> *Can you imagine using your grandfather's science book? It would be out of date, wouldn't it!*
>
> *But the Bible is **never** outdated. Every word of it is true!*

The Bible has not changed and never will change because God is its author.

 READ Psalm 119:89.

J. The Bible is God's personal message to each of us; it is the most important message we will ever be given.

Why is it so important for you and me to study the Bible?

The Bible is special — it is different from any other book.

— The Bible tells us about God.

— The Bible tells us what God thinks of us and what He sees as our greatest need.

The Bible is important because it is God's personal message to each one of us!

— Boys and girls, dads and moms, grandmas and grandpas, **all people everywhere** — God wrote the Bible to each one of us personally.

K. Conclusion:

The Bible has been printed more times and translated into more languages than any other book in the whole world. More lives have been changed by the Bible than by any other book! [13]

The Bible is also **God's personal message to us**. He wrote it to communicate with people — with you and with me.

If someone wrote you a letter, what would you do? You would read it, wouldn't you!

[Hold up your Bible] This Bible is God's letter to you and to me. Let's study God's Word together and find out what it says!

[13] In the book, *From God to Us: How We Got Our Bible*, the authors open by saying that the Bible is "the most quoted, the most published, the most translated, and the most influential book in the history of mankind."

From God to Us: How We Got Our Bible, by Norman L. Geisler and William E. Nix, Moody Press, Chicago, 1974, p. 7. ❏

QUESTIONS:

1. God chose men to write down His Words. What are these men called? *Prophets.*

2. How many years passed before all of God's Word was written down? *It took about 1,600 years before all of God's words were written.*

3. How many men were there whom God used to write down His Word? *Approximately forty.*

4. What nationality were they? *They were all Jewish, except one man. (Luke was a Gentile.)*

5. Did they write God's words in English? *No. (They were written in Hebrew, Greek, and Aramaic.)*

6. Who is the author of the Bible? *God.*

7. Why should a person study the Bible? *The Bible is God's personal message to every individual.*

LESSON 1 — Suggestions for Activities

Be sure to allow time to teach the lesson first!

Listed below are carefully designed activities which will help reinforce and focus on the themes you have taught in the lesson. Choose from this list whatever best suits your students and prepare ahead accordingly. The children may participate in these activities during the time remaining after the lesson has been taught.

1. **Memory Verse — II Timothy 3:16**

   Provide materials for the children to make memory verse reminders to take home. You will need a strip of heavy paper and two pencils for each child.

   Have each child copy II Timothy 3:16 on his/her strip of paper. (To save class time, you may wish to type or write the verse on the strips of paper beforehand.) Have the children make scrolls by attaching the ends of their strips of paper to the pencils (with tape or glue). Show the children how to roll their papers into scrolls, starting from the ends and working toward the middle.

   Reinforce that the Bible is God's message to mankind.

2. **God's Word Written**

   Provide each child with a copy of Chronological Drawing No. 1.

   Have them color their drawing and write out their memory verse on the bottom of it.

   Reinforce that God told men called "prophets" the exact messages that He wanted written down. God communicates with man.

3. **God's Word Translated**

   Bring to class Bibles in other languages, such as Spanish or German. (If you know of a missionary or mission agency, ask to borrow a Bible or portion of a Bible translation that the missionaries have done for a special language group.) If you don't have a Bible in another language, you could bring a copy of a verse or verses in other languages.

   Explain: "God has enabled men to translate the Bible into many languages. The Bible has been translated into more languages than any other book. Let's look at some translations of the Bible in other languages."

   As the children look at the different translations, emphasize that the Bible is God's message to the whole world.

4. **God's Message for the World**

   Write the following incomplete sentences on a poster:

   1) God gave His message through _____.

   2) God's message is for _____.

   3) God's message is for _____.

   On individual strips of paper, write the answers:

   1) the Jewish people.

   2) the whole world.

   3) ME!

   Have the children glue the individual strips on the poster to complete the sentences.

   Reinforce that the Bible is God's personal message to each one of us.

5. **Explore Your Bible**

   Spend time helping the children learn how to find verses in the Bible. Go through the steps of finding a verse with them: Review the Table of Contents, showing them how to find the page on which a book of the Bible starts. Then help them see how to find a chapter, by looking at the top of the page in their Bible. Then help them learn to find the verse. Have them look up different verses (chosen from the lesson) for practice.

   Some of your students may already be familiar with their Bibles. Encourage them to help others in the class. Explain that you are not so much interested in who can find it first as you are in everyone finding the verse.

   Help the children explore the other resources in their Bibles, such as maps, concordance, etc.

6. **Match the Numbers**

   On the blackboard or a piece of poster paper list the following numbers and words. (The words below are beside the number with which they go, but when putting them on the blackboard for the children, mix up the words.) Have the children draw lines to connect the correct number and word.

40	men
1,600	years
1	Author

   Emphasize that although 40 men wrote down the Bible over a period of 1,600 years, every word was authored by God.

Name _____

The Bible is GOD's Word!

God spoke His Word to men called prophets

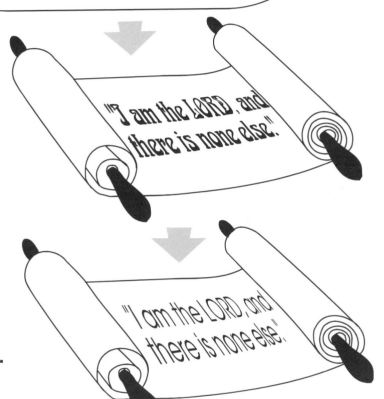

"I am the LORD, and there is none else."

God's prophets wrote down exactly what God wanted them to write.

When the scrolls wore out from use, new copies were made very carefully.

God's Word has been accurately translated into many languages.

Our Bible is truly **GOD'S WORD!**

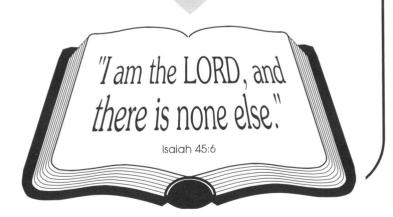

"*I am the LORD, and there is none else.*"

Isaiah 45:6

skit 1 Introducing the Bible

Readers: Uncle Don, Travis, Jessica

Uncle Don:
Hi, Jessica. Hi, Travis. What are you doing today?

Travis:
We're bored.

Jessica:
Mom said we could come over and visit you for a minute if we don't bother you.

Uncle Don:
You're not a bother. I'm glad to have you. It's not every uncle that has his niece and nephew right next door! I'm glad you moved here — especially since your dad is travelling so much now.

Travis:
I like coming over here to see you.

Jessica:
I know you! You like the cookies and milk he gives us!

Travis:
You're right!

Uncle Don:
I just happen to have some more cookies. I'll get some for us.

Travis:
Uncle Don, what were you reading?

Jessica:
That's his Bible. Don't you know? He reads his Bible a lot — don't you, Uncle Don.

Uncle Don:
Yes, Jessica, I do. It's the greatest of all books.

Travis:
What's so great about it?

Uncle Don:
It's God's book — God is the author of the Bible.

Travis:
Do you mean that He wrote it?

Uncle Don:
He had men write down His Words. The Bible is God's personal message to each one of us.

Jessica:
To us? I thought it was written a long time ago.

Uncle Don:
It was. Actually, God used over 40 men to write down all His Words. And it was written over a period of 1,600 years.

Travis:
1,600 years? You must be kidding!

Uncle Don:
No, God had men write down His messages for years and years until everything was written down that He wanted to tell us. The Bible is the greatest and most accurate of all history books. But better than that, the Bible is God's story.

Jessica:
You mean it is about Him?

Uncle Don:
Yes, Jessica, God is the One whom the Bible is all about. It's not just history; it's HIS STORY!

Travis:
The Bible is an awfully big book. I don't know how anyone could ever read it all.

Uncle Don:
You'd be surprised. I've read it through many times, and each time I enjoy it more and want to read it more.

Travis:
You mean you've actually read that whole big book lots of times? Why?

Uncle Don:
Travis, the Bible has the answers for all the important questions of life. The Bible never changes, because God never changes. Everything He had written down thousands of years ago is still useful to us today.

Jessica:
You mean it's not just a bunch of old stories?

Uncle Don:
Absolutely not. Everything recorded in the Bible is true. And everything recorded there is for us to know. God wants us to know Him.

Travis:
You mean, like we know a person?

Uncle Don:
Yes, only God is greater than anyone. You really can get to know Him. How would you kids like to start to learn about God?

Jessica:
I'd like to.

Travis:
Me, too.

Uncle Don:
First we'll need to check with your mom, to make sure it's okay with her. Then we can set up a time to meet and study the Bible together. I think you'll be surprised how much you will learn and how much sense it will make to you.

Bible Stories We Will Study on the Time Line of History

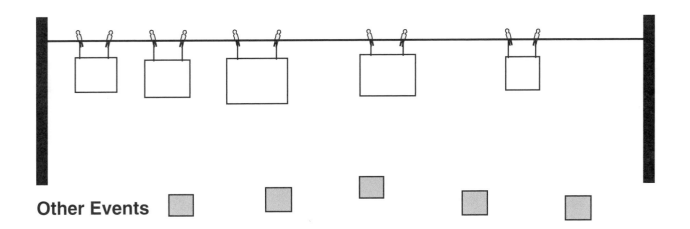

Other Events

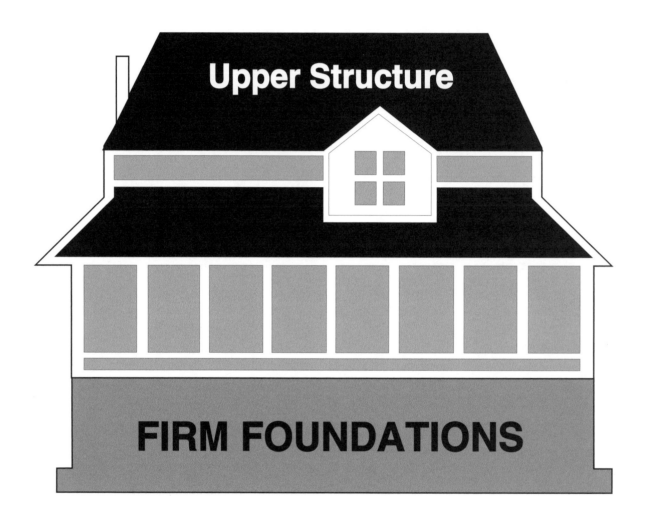

Upper Structure

FIRM FOUNDATIONS

GOD'S WORD

ISRAEL

THE WHOLE WORLD

FIRM FOUNDATIONS **VISUAL**

God Alone

Job 38:4

Psalm
50:21;
90:2

Isaiah
43:10;
46:9,10;
55:8,9

Colos-
sians
1:17

Hebrews
1:10-12

Revela-
tion
1:8

LESSON PREPARATION
This section is for you, the teacher.

The passages in the Scripture Reference column are for your own study in preparing for this lesson. Since they may contain concepts that run ahead of the lesson, they are not to be taught at this point.

Note: If you have not taught previously from this series of lessons, please read carefully the note to teachers in the front of this book.

SCRIPTURE: Genesis 1:1

LESSON GOALS:

- To present the fact of God's existence before all things.
- To establish the fact of God's sovereignty. [1]

THIS LESSON SHOULD HELP THE CHILDREN:

- To have an increased awe of God .
- To consider God's account of the beginning.

Daniel
11:36;
12:4

The
Trinity:

Genesis
1:1, 2;
1:26;
3:22

Matthew
28:17-19

Romans
8:26, 34

II Corinthi-
ans
13:14

Ephesians
1:17;
2:13,18

Hebrews
9:14

PERSPECTIVE FOR THE TEACHER:

In our culture, self is exalted and assigned that place of control and supremacy that belongs to God alone.[2] Here are just a few of the evidences of this self-centered thinking: People in our country spend millions of dollars every year to improve their self-image and to try to exert more control over their lives and over the world around them. At every turn, men are seeking knowledge and boasting of their discoveries as if they had originated life and the laws that control the universe. To be anything but the best and the one in control of one's own destiny seems unthinkable in our culture. Our schools are being swiftly and subtly taken over by humanistic philosophies that put man in the place of God. Many children are being bombarded daily with this kind of teaching.

In sharp contrast, this lesson is filled with foundational insights into the character and attributes of God. All other spiritual understanding begins here. Without these truths, no one can correctly assess his own life or the world around him.

Pray that the children will hear, recognize, and welcome the truth and begin to embrace the fact of God's sovereignty.

INTRODUCING THE TRINITY:

Point D of the lesson outline introduces that God is a Trinity. The word Trinity does not appear in Scripture, but the fact of the Trinity is evident from Genesis to Revelation. (The Scripture Reference column gives some examples.)

The Trinity is introduced at this point in the lessons because:

1. The Trinity is eternal and, chronologically, existed before the beginning.
2. The word God in Genesis 1:1 is the Hebrew word *Elohim*. Because of its ending, *Elohim* is a plural name with a singular meaning (indicated by the

OVERVIEW

This lesson begins to lay the foundational truth of God's sovereignty by showing that God existed alone before the beginning and that He exists independently of all else and needs nothing. It gives a very brief introduction to the Trinity.

It also establishes the fact that because God was the only One there before the beginning, He alone can tell us what happened in the beginning.

MEMORY
VERSE
Psalm 90:2

[1] In presenting His sovereignty, we will be introducing several characteristics and attributes of God: He is eternal and present everywhere: He is Spirit: He is a Trinity.

We will use a few selected verses to establish these points. But remember, this study is **foundational. Keep it simple.** Let the Word do its work in hearts by carefully planting God's Word, a little at a time. ❏

[2] Be alert to your students' comments and questions. Their responses to the lesson will begin to reveal their understanding of God. ❏

fact that it is used with singular verbs). This suggests the uni-plurality of the Godhead.

3. God the Son was there in the beginning. He is included with God the Father and God the Holy Spirit in the words, *"In the beginning God created the heaven and the earth."*

4. If we fail to teach the Trinity in the beginning and throughout the Old Testament, it will be more difficult to teach the deity of Jesus when we come to the story of His birth. It is much easier for us to teach and for our students to understand if we have taught — from the beginning — that Jesus was forever coequal with the Father, active in creation, and in the entire Old Testament story. A statement such as, *"...Before Abraham was, I am"* (John 8:58), will be less difficult for the children to understand if we have taught them that God the Son was there, even before the beginning.

   NOTE: We will not use His name, Jesus, or His title, Christ, while teaching the Old Testament. Both are connected with His earthly ministry. Refer to Him only as God the Son during the Old Testament teaching.

5. Since the Holy Spirit is mentioned in the Old Testament, the subject of the Trinity cannot be avoided (Genesis 1:2, cf. 6:3).

6. Genesis 1:26 uses the plurals "us" and "our."

   Do not try to explain the Trinity. It is impossible, and all illustrations (e.g., water, egg, triangle) fall far short of the truth. It is better to admit that we cannot understand the Trinity.

John 1:1-3

VISUALS:

- Chart 2, "GOD IS GREATER THAN ALL!"
- Visual, "The Bible Is HIS STORY"
- Poster 1, "LEARNING ABOUT GOD"
- Chronological Chart No. 1

SPECIAL PREPARATION:

- Make copies for your class of the **Lesson 2 Review Sheet** and **Skit 2** (at the end of this lesson). Provide pencils for the children.
- Photocopy **visual** (at end of lesson) — use as small poster or for overhead transparency.
- Prepare for any activity you select from the **Suggestions for Activities** (at the end of this lesson). As you select activities, remember to allow sufficient time to teach the outlined lesson material.

ON TEACHING THIS LESSON:

You are carefully laying a scriptural foundation on which the Gospel will later be presented. Each lesson builds on previous lessons, so be sure to cover each point carefully.

DON'T COMPLICATE THE MESSAGE!

As you teach, keep in mind that this is a directed study — not an exhaustive survey of the Bible. Keep your lesson on track and moving ahead by limiting and directing any discussion.

Carefully follow the outline. Emphasize the doctrinal themes.

LESSON FORMAT: The **center column** below contains the lesson material to be taught to the students. The **bold outline headings** are only for reference and need not be spoken, as they are incorporated into the outlined material that follows. The material in the **side columns** is for the teacher's own reference and is not intended to be included in the lesson.

TO BE TAUGHT TO THE STUDENTS
(Center Column Only)

LESSON OUTLINE:

REVIEW Lesson 1, using the Lesson 2 Review Sheet.
PERFORM Skit 2. Note: "Uncle Don's" part should be read by an adult.

A. Introduction

Who is God?

What is He like?

How can we know Him?

In our first lesson we said that God is the main character, the central focus, of the Bible.

— He is the One who gave the Bible to us.

— The Bible is a book of true history — history from God's point of view.

— It is God's story, or, as someone has so correctly said, the Bible is "HIS STORY."

Suggested Visual:

> **The Bible is**
> # HIS STORY

We are going to learn about God from God Himself.

We will study what He has said about Himself in His Word.

— Why should we study about God? Because **He wants us to know Him!**

— Of all the things we can study, learning about God is the very best!

— In Jeremiah 9:23,24 God says, *"Thus saith the LORD, Let not the wise man glory in his wisdom, neither let the mighty man glory in his might, let not the rich man glory in his riches:* **But let him that glorieth glory in this, that he understandeth and knoweth me, that I am the LORD...."** [3]

This verse tells us that knowing God is the most important thing we can do.

How great is God?

— How important is He?

— Did He have a beginning?

— Will He have an end?

— Where did He come from?

— What does God need?

Let's open our Bibles and see how God answers these questions in His Word.

B. Only God is eternal. All else has a beginning.

 **READ Genesis 1:1.**

[3] The teacher reads this verse in part because the rest of it (not printed here) contains themes that run ahead of the lesson. The words in bold type are what you want to emphasize. ❏

4 Genesis is the foundation for all the Scripture, and Genesis 1 is the foundation for Genesis. Do not rush through Genesis 1 because the basic revelations of the nature and character of God are presented in it. ❑

The first words God wrote for us in the Bible are, *"In the beginning..."* (Genesis 1:1). **4**

— God gave us these words so that we would know there was a beginning to all things.

— Everything that we can see and everything that we know about but can't see had a beginning, except God Himself.

— Before the beginning, there was:

No universe

No earth

No angels

No devil

No plants

No animals

No people.

— All these had beginnings.

C. God alone had no beginning; God will have no end; God is ETERNAL.

 Theme: God is greater than all and more important than all; He is the highest authority.

Before anything came to be, God existed as He does now and will forever.

We're going to look at a chart which lists some things about God and about man. We'll begin with this: **5**

POINT TO THE CHART AND READ:

5 The statements about man are read without comment. They are just there to make your students consider God's greatness and to prepare their minds for later studies. ❑

GOD	MAN
GOD had no beginning will have no end.	MAN is born and dies.

 READ Psalm 90:2. [Have all the children read this verse together, several times.]

— There never was a time when God did not exist.

He did not have a beginning.

He was not created.

He has always been alive.

He has always been and will always be the same.

There never will be a time when God does not exist.

God can never die — He is eternal — He is forever!

POINT TO THE POSTER, "LEARNING ABOUT GOD." READ, "God had no beginning and He will never end — He is eternal."

D. God is a Trinity. **6**

6 As mentioned in the introduction, do not try to explain the Trinity.

This subject may stir up questions, and some students will have a hard time waiting until later lessons for answers. As tactfully as you can, try to assure them that their questions are good, but that you must wait to answer them. ❑

SHOW CHRONOLOGICAL CHART DISPLAYING THE WORDS: GOD — FATHER, SON, HOLY SPIRIT.

God is forever, eternally one God.

But look at Genesis 1:26: *"And God said, Let **us** make man in **our** image, after **our** likeness...."* **7**

We aren't going to study this verse right now; we just want to look at the words "us" and "our." [Make sure the children all find this verse.]

As we study God's Word, we will discover that, although there is only one God, there are three persons who are equally God.

Who are these three persons?

All of the three are named in Matthew 28:19: [7]

— God the Father

— God the Son

— God the Holy Spirit ("Holy Ghost" means "Holy Spirit").

POINT TO CHRONOLOGICAL CHART NO. 1, SHOWING GOD — FATHER, SON, HOLY SPIRIT.

We use the word "Trinity" to describe these three persons who are the one Eternal God.

— Define:
The word "Trinity" is made from "tri-," meaning three (as in "tricycle") and "unit," meaning one — that is, three-in-one.

POINT TO THE CHART AND READ:

GOD is a Trinity of three persons.	**MAN is only one person.**

There is the Father who is God, the Son who is God, and the Holy Spirit who is God.

Hard to understand? Yes, to us it certainly is!

God is so much greater than we can imagine.

— The Trinity is beyond our understanding.

— We can only describe what we understand from God's Word.

The amazing fact of the Trinity is just one of the things that shows us the greatness of God!

— Consider:
Can you describe gravity? No! Even the scientists don't really understand it! But we can see what it does. That's how it is with God. We can see what He does and learn about Him from His Word. But He is far above our ability to understand.

E. Because God alone existed before all things, God is completely independent of everything and everyone.

Theme: God is greater than all and more important than all; He is the highest authority.

Because God existed before all things, we know that He didn't need anything.

— God was there alone, before the earth, the sun, the moon, the stars, the galaxies.

He does not need the earth nor anything on it.

— He doesn't need air to breathe.

— He doesn't need food to eat.

— He doesn't need water to drink.

[7] Be careful to stick to the subject here. Both of these verses, Genesis 1:26 and Matthew 28:19, are used only to show specific words. Don't get sidetracked into the subject of the verses themselves. ❏

God does not need the sun.

— He can see perfectly without any light.

— He doesn't need to sleep; He has no need of day or night.

God doesn't need any source of energy.

— He never gets tired, thirsty, or hungry.

God doesn't need **anything!**

POINT TO THE CHART AND READ:

GOD needs nothing.	**MAN needs food, water, air, sleep light, protection, etc.**

God doesn't even need anyone to teach Him.

— He knows everything; He has all knowledge.

— He is aware of everything.

 READ Psalm 147:5: *"Great is our Lord, and of great power: **his understanding is infinite.**"*

Infinite means "without end."

 READ Romans 11:33,34.

POINT TO THE CHART AND READ:

GOD knows everything	**MAN needs to be taught.**

What about us?

— Could we have been born into the world without parents?

Could we have survived as little babies without care?

Could we have learned to read and write without someone to teach us?

— What about our bodies?

How long could we live without food and water? [Only a few days or perhaps a week without water!]

How long could we live without oxygen? [Only a few minutes!]

How many days could we live without sleep?

How long could we survive without protection against the sun's ultraviolet rays?

— Example:

Astronauts wear special suits when they leave the protection of the earth's atmosphere. If they weren't protected, they would die immediately from lack of oxygen and from exposure to the sun's ultraviolet rays.

— In order to live, we must have food, water, sleep, oxygen, and protection from ultraviolet rays, cold, heat, and many other things; and we must be taught everything.

— But God does not need anything or any person!

F. God is Spirit.

God does not need the earth to live on and the many other things which we humans need because God does not have a body as we do.

John 4:24 says that *"God is a Spirit."* **8**

— God does not have flesh and bones like humans, animals, birds, or reptiles.

— Because He does not have a material body, He does not have bodily needs.

POINT TO THE CHART AND READ:

GOD is Spirit and has no material body.	**MAN has a material body.**

It is important for us to remember the fact that God is Spirit.

He is not just a force, as some would describe Him.

No, God is Spirit, a Trinity of three persons, all with mind, personality, and will.

He is the God who has personally given us His Word so we can know Him.

God is so great!

G. God is in all places at the same time.

 Theme: God is everywhere all the time.

 Theme: God is greater than all and more important than all; He is the highest authority.

Where is God?

Where was He before everything else existed?

We cannot see God, and we couldn't know where He is unless He had told us.

— In the Bible, God tells us He is **everywhere all the time!**

— He is **not** in everything that is, everything is not God. **9**

— He is the Creator, separate from and greater than all His creation.
    God is higher than all.
    God is greater than all He has made.

— God fills the universe.

 READ Jeremiah 23:23,24.

— He is in all places on the earth.

— God is here right now and can see us all.

POINT TO THE POSTER, "LEARNING ABOUT GOD." READ, "God is everywhere all the time; He knows everything. "

— Illustration:
Have you ever wanted to be in two places at the same time? Maybe you wanted to go somewhere with your family and you also wanted to stay and play a game with your friend. But you couldn't do that. You and I and all people can only be in one place at a time. But God is everywhere, all the time!

— Note:
One little boy, when hearing this about God, said, God is so big He doesn't have to go anywhere!

8 The teacher reads this verse only in part because the rest of the verse (not printed here) contains themes not covered in these lessons. Be sure to keep the lesson on track. Stick to the main themes. ❏

9 Be certain that you make a clear distinction between God the Creator and His creation. Pantheistic religions (such as New Age) believe that god is everything and everything is god. Sadly, some of the children may already have been exposed to this teaching.

(Do not get into a discussion on creation here; it is simply mentioned to clarify the point of God's sovereignty.) ❏

POINT TO THE CHART AND READ:

GOD is everywhere all the time.	MAN is only in one place at a time.

— God and God alone is able to be everywhere all the time. Since God is everywhere all the time, is there any place you can be or go where He is not? [10]

  Is there any place you can "hide" from God?

 READ Psalm 139:7-12.

H. God alone was before all things; He alone is greater than all; God is SOVEREIGN.

God is beyond our understanding:

AS YOU TEACH, POINT TO THE CHART, "GOD IS GREATER THAN ALL."

— We cannot understand One who had no beginning and will have no end.

— We cannot imagine one God who is three persons.

— We cannot understand One who is never in need of anything.

— We have never met anyone who knows everything.

— We cannot see One who is Spirit.

— We are unable to know what it is like to be everywhere at the same time.

READ Jeremiah 10:6.

We must simply admit that there is One who is truly greater than all and higher than all.

POINT TO THE POSTER, "LEARNING ABOUT GOD." READ, "God is greater than all and more important than all; He is the highest authority."

The way we describe God's greatness is to say that God is SOVEREIGN. [Write this word on the board and have the children say it.]

— Webster's Dictionary says that "sovereign" means "ruler, supreme in power, chief, effective in highest degree...."

— The Bible often refers to God as "The Most High."

— Psalm 83:18 calls God *"the most high over all the earth."*

— In Isaiah 45:5, God says, *"I am the LORD, and there is none else, there is no God beside me...."*

POINT TO THE CHART AND READ: [11]

GOD is greater than all and more important than all, He is the highest authority.	MAN should be under God's authority and listen to everything God says.

Proverbs
15:3

Romans
11:33-36

10 Some of your students may think that Satan can be everywhere, all the time. He cannot, though he has many demons spread over the earth. Each demon, also, can only be in one place at one time.

At this time, avoid getting into a discussion on Satan and his demons, as this will be addressed in the next lesson. ❏

11 Again, it is not necessary to comment on the note about man. ❏

I. God alone can tell us about the beginning.

Theme: God is greater than all and more important than all; He is the highest authority.

Only God was there in the beginning!

POINT TO THE CHART AND READ:

GOD was there before the beginning of everything.	MAN was not there before the beginning.

He knows about the beginning of everything.
And in the Bible He has given us the record of all beginnings.

Only God was there and only He can tell us exactly what happened.

In the lessons to come we will be reading God's record of the beginning of everything.

J. Conclusion

No, we cannot really understand how great God is.

But we can learn a great deal about Him!

And these are things God wants us to know and remember! God is far greater than we can imagine:

— He is truly greater than all.

— He is sovereign — the highest ruler.

He alone had no beginning.

He will have no end.

He is a Trinity, the great God who is three in one: God the Father, God the Son, and God the Holy Spirit.

He needs nothing.

He has no bodily needs because He is Spirit.

He knows everything.

He is in all places at the same time.

God is the most important of all; He is the greatest!

QUESTIONS

1. Was there ever a time when God was not living? *No.*
2. What does God need in order to exist? *God doesn't need anything.*
3. Does God have a body? *No.*
4. How many Gods are there? *There is only one God.*
5. Who are the three living beings who are the one God? *God the Father, God the Son, and God the Holy Spirit.*
6. Is there some faraway place you could go on this earth or in this galaxy or this universe or anywhere that God would not be? *No.*
7. What do we mean when we say that God is sovereign? *He alone is ruler; He is greater than all and more important than all; He is the Most High.*

LESSON 2 — Suggestions for Activities

Be sure to allow time to teach the lesson first!

Listed below are carefully designed activities which will help reinforce and focus on the themes you have taught in the lesson. Choose from this list whatever best suits your students and prepare ahead accordingly. The children may participate in these activities during the time remaining after the lesson has been taught.

1. **Memory Verse — Psalm 90:2**

   Provide art supplies so the children can draw a picture reminder of their memory verse.

   Have them draw pictures of mountains (or the world) as a background on which they write out their memory verse.

2. **Before the Beginning**

   Before class, prepare a poster with 2 columns, labeled as shown below. Write each word shown in the columns on individual strips of paper. The children will glue these on during class. Use bright, bold lettering for "Only God" so it will stand out on the poster. (Note: This activity can be done with children who do not yet read by using pictures where possible and reading the other words for them.)

Has Always Existed	Had a Beginning
ONLY GOD	Universe
	Earth
	Sun
	Moon
	Stars
	Angels
	Devil
	Plants
	Animals
	People

   Explain to the children that each word strip should be placed under one of the two columns. Without telling the children, pass out only the word strips under the column "Had a Beginning." Have the children take turns gluing the word strips to the right column.

   After all the words in the column "Had a Beginning" are glued on, ask the children what words could go under the column "Has Always Existed." Choose a child to glue the bold, bright word strip, "Only God," in the correct column.

   Emphasize that God is eternal.

3. **God Is Spirit**

   This activity is designed to help the children realize that although man needs many things, God does not need anything.

   Prepare flash card pictures showing some of the things that people need in order to survive, such as a person eating, sleeping, being taught, etc.

   Holding up one flash card at a time, discuss with the children what people need and explain that God does not need these things because God is Spirit. For example, hold up the flash card of a person eating. Ask the children, "What is this person doing? Why is he eating? Do you think a person could live very long if he didn't eat? People need to eat food, don't they? Does God need food to eat? Why not?"

   As you discuss each flash card, emphasize that God does not need the things that people need because God does not have a human body. Reinforce that God is Spirit.

4. **God Is Everywhere All the Time**

   This activity will make personal to the children the truth that God is in all places all the time. He is not just out there somewhere; He is ever-present, everywhere they go.

   Provide art supplies for the children. Explain: "We learned in our lesson that God is in all places at the same time. Jeremiah 23:23-24 says that God fills heaven and earth. Psalm 139 says no one can hide from God's presence because God is everywhere — He is in the heaven, the sea, the night, etc. We are going to draw some of the places where God is. Because you can't really draw a picture that shows `everywhere,' let's each choose one specific place to draw, someplace different from what everyone else is drawing. Susie, why don't you draw a picture of the stars. Tony, you draw a picture of your school. (Continue giving them suggestions or let them suggest ideas. Be sure to assign some children to draw pictures of places they are familiar with, such as their home, the local park, the grocery store, etc.) Now remember, God is everywhere all the time. He doesn't need to go from one place to another; He actually fills the universe. God is in all these places you are drawing, and He is there all the time. Isn't God awesome!"

   Make a collage of the children's drawings on the wall. Point to the different pictures and remind the children that God is in each place all at the same time.

5. **Check the Dictionary**

   Provide a dictionary so the children can look up several of the words you have discussed in the lesson.

   Have the children look up the words "sovereign," "eternal," and "trinity." As you discuss the meaning of the words with the children, reinforce these attributes of God.

Name _____

The Bible is the Word of God

Write out II Timothy 3:16 and memorize it.

_____

_____

_____

_____

_____

_____

Use this WORD BANK to fill in the blanks to the questions below. Cross out each word on the list as you use it so you can see what is left.

WORD BANK: God   1,600   Jewish   40   communicates   prophets

---

1. When God wanted His words written down, He chose men to write them. He put into their minds the exact words He wanted written. These men who wrote down God's Word are called _____.

2. These men lived at different times and in different places. As a matter of fact, it took about _____ years before all of God's Word was written down.

3. God used about _____ men to write His Word.

4. All but one of them were of the same nationality — they were _____. (Luke was a Gentile — not a Jew.)

5. Who is the author of the Bible? _____

6. The Bible is God's personal message to every one of us! God _____ with us! He tells us what we need to know.

LESSON 2 FIRM FOUNDATIONS **REVIEW SHEET**

skit 2 God Alone

Readers: Uncle Don, Travis, Jessica

Travis:
Guess what, Uncle Don! We're going to go camping next weekend!

Jessica:
You should see all the stuff we're taking.

Travis:
I even got a new flashlight!

Jessica:
And I got a sleeping bag!

Travis:
I already had one for scouts.

Jessica:
There are three families going from where Mom works. Everybody is bringing part of the food. All Mom has to bring is desserts.

Travis:
I hope she brings a lot!

Jessica:
Oh, Travis! You're **always** hungry!

Uncle Don:
Where are you going?

Travis:
Up to the lake.

Uncle Don:
That's a beautiful place. But you sure do have to bring in everything you'll need. There's nothing up there but the trees and the water — no stores or houses.

Jessica:
I never realized how much stuff we do need!

Uncle Don:
You're right, Jessica. We really do need a lot just to live. Of course, most of us have more than we really need. Did you ever stop to think that God doesn't need **anything**?

Jessica:
What do you mean, Uncle Don?

Uncle Don:
Just exactly that — God doesn't need anything. God has always been and always will be. He existed before anything was created. He was there before there was any light or air or food or water; He existed before the angels!

Travis:
But didn't God have a beginning sometime?

Uncle Don:
No, God is eternal — He had no beginning and He will have no end.

Travis:
How can that be?

Uncle Don:
God is greater than our understanding. God is greater than all! The very first words in the Bible are "In the beginning, God . . . ."

Jessica:
So He was there in the beginning?

Uncle Don:
God was there **before** the beginning.

Travis:
But where did He come from?

Uncle Don:
That's the exciting part, Travis. Everything else had a beginning. **God had no beginning**. He simply **IS**, eternally. And He doesn't need **anything**.

Jessica:
Doesn't he need people?

Uncle Don:
No, Jessica. There was a time when nothing existed but God. No air, no light, no people — nothing but God.

Travis:
Wasn't God lonely?

Uncle Don:
No, God is very, very special. The Bible tells us that He is really three persons in one. We call God a "Trinity." We can't begin to understand how wonderful He is. God the Father, God the Son, and God the Holy Spirit — who are together the One great God — have existed forever.

Travis:
Now I am confused.

Uncle Don:
You know, Travis, I don't even **try** to understand some things about God — I just accept them by faith. He is so much greater than anyone can ever imagine! God is not like us. But we **can** know a lot about Him, just by studying His Word, the Bible. God is truly wonderful, and **He wants us to know Him!**

Jessica:
Mom said that Travis and I could study the Bible with you.

Uncle Don:
Yes, I talked with her, too. I'm eager to start. Let's start right here at the beginning, with that verse I told you about in Genesis 1:1.

The Bible Is

HIS STORY

lesson
3 God Created the Spirit Beings:
Lucifer Rebelled

Isaiah
14:12-20

Ezekiel
28:11-18

Romans
8:37-39

Ephesians
6:10-18

LESSON PREPARATION

This section is for you, the teacher.

The passages in the Scripture Reference column are for your own study in preparing for this lesson. Since they may contain concepts that run ahead of the lesson, they are not to be taught at this point.

Note: If you have not taught previously from this series of lessons, please read carefully the note to teachers in the front of this book.

LESSON GOALS:

- To show the sovereignty and holiness of God in His creation of the spirits and in His dealing with Lucifer and the other spirits who rebelled.

THIS LESSON SHOULD HELP THE STUDENTS:

- To see that God is greater than all and more powerful than all.
- To see the seriousness of rebellion against God.

PERSPECTIVE FOR THE TEACHER:

In our society, Satan has been given increasing attention in films, books, music, games, etc. People from all economic levels and backgrounds have become involved in satanic-oriented practices. II Corinthians 11:14 says that Satan masquerades as an angel of light. The Enemy's subtlety has fooled some (like Eve), while others have simply made knowing steps of rebellion (like Adam).

Children need to know the truth. God is the sovereign Creator; Satan is a created being who lost his postition as God's servant. Rather than frighten the children, this truth will give them stability and understanding. **Throughout the lesson, emphasize God's greatness and superiority — His sovereignty.**

As this lesson is studied, you may find that your students have many questions. You may even find that some of the children and/or their families are involved in satanic things, such as (to name only a few), horoscopes, ouija boards, mediums, seances, satanic games, or rock music with filthy words. Anything that causes people to search for answers or power from any source other than God, is of Satan. Satan is a liar, a thief, a deceiver, an accuser, and a murderer. He wants to deceive as many as possible so they will not listen to God's Word and believe.

Jeremiah
32:27

Matthew
16:18

Revela-
tion
1:8

But remember: no matter what opposition we face to the message of the Bible; no matter what difficulties, entanglements, and sins may be manifest in our students, we have assurance in God's Word that He is stronger than all. Nothing is too hard for Him. God will use His Word in hearts and will give you wisdom in dealing with your students. Our Enemy is strong, but OUR GOD IS STRONGER THAN ALL! In Jesus Christ, we have victory.

NOTE:

Before we teach how God created all the material things which can be seen, we will first teach that God created the spirit world which generally cannot be seen. It is best to teach about the spirits and Satan at this stage because:

1. All spirits — that is, all angels — witnessed the creation of the earth (Job 38:4-7).

OVERVIEW

This lesson establishes that God created all the spirit beings. It presents God who is sovereign and holy, greater than all created beings, creating all things perfect. It also shows God's sovereignty and holiness in dealing with Lucifer's willful rebellion against God.

MEMORY VERSE Psalm 90:2*

* This important verse is repeated from Lesson 2.

2. It is much easier for both teacher and learner if each actor is introduced into the story at the time of his creation or birth, rather than the teacher having to return to an earlier point in the story to fill in the gaps.

3. The story of Genesis 3 is complicated enough in itself, without adding the teaching of the creation and fall of Satan and his hosts.

The Bible does not give a clear chronology of the fall of Satan. For this reason, theologians have often come to differing conclusions regarding whether this took place before, after, or during the creation of the world. (Many point to Genesis 1:31, *"And God saw everything that he had made, and, behold, it was very good"* to support the view that all the spirit beings were still in their original, perfect state at this point.) In these lessons we will not deal with this issue, as it is not critical to a foundational understanding of the Word.

Two of the key Old Testament passages relating to the doctrine of Satan are Isaiah 14:12-20 and Ezekiel 28:11-18. These are used carefully in the outline because they are difficult passages to interpret, since they also contain prophecy pertaining to men. **Limit any discussion to the subject at hand.**

A good source of Scriptures relating to angels and to Satan and demons is Vine's *Expository Dictionary of New Testament Words*.[1] This is just a quick reference; obviously, more comprehensive studies and books are available.

[1] *An Expository Dictionary of New Testament Words*, W. E. Vine, Fleming H. Revell Co., 1966

VISUALS:

- Chronological Chart
- Poster 1, "Learning About God" — Use this poster to emphasize attributes already introduced, and to introduce additional attributes as noted in the instructions in the outline.
- Visual, "Angels"
- Visual, "To Rebel"

SPECIAL PREPARATION

- Make copies for your class of the **Lesson 3 Review Sheet** and **Skit 3** (at the end of this lesson). Provide pencils for the children.
- Photocopy **visuals** (at end of lesson) — use as small posters or for overhead transparencies.
- Prepare for any activity you select from the **Suggestions for Activities** (at the end of this lesson). As you select activities, remember to allow sufficient time to teach the outlined lesson material.

LOOKING AHEAD

- Begin collecting pictures for Lesson 5 (See Lesson 5, Special Preparation).

ON TEACHING THIS LESSON:

You are carefully laying a scriptural foundation on which the Gospel will later be presented. Each lesson builds on previous lessons, so be sure to cover each point carefully.

DON'T COMPLICATE THE MESSAGE!

As you teach, keep in mind that this is a directed study — not an exhaustive survey of the Bible. Keep your lesson on track and moving ahead by limiting and directing any discussion.

Carefully follow the outline. Emphasize the doctrinal themes.

LESSON FORMAT: The **center column** below contains the lesson material to be taught to the students. The **bold outline headings** are only for reference and need not be spoken, as they are incorporated into the outlined material that follows. The material in the **side columns** is for the teacher's own reference and is not intended to be included in the lesson.

TO BE TAUGHT TO THE STUDENTS
(Center Column Only)

LESSON OUTLINE:

REVIEW Lesson 2, using the Lesson 3 Review sheet.

PERFORM Skit 3. Note: Uncle Don's part should be read by an adult.

A. Introduction

Have you ever wondered:

— Where did the angels come from?

— What about Satan — where did he come from?

Who can tell us?

Only God can; and He has, in His Word!

B. God created all of the spirits.

SHOW CHRONOLOGICAL CHART DISPLAYING THE WORDS: GOD'S ANGELS, LUCIFER.

John 1:3

Colos-
sians
1:16

 Theme: God is greater than all and more important than all; He is the highest authority.

In the beginning, **God created** all of the spirit beings.

— The Bible uses many different words to talk about the spirit beings:

> Spirits
>
> Angels
>
> Cherubim
>
> Seraphim
>
> The host of the Lord or host of Heaven
>
> Powers
>
> Principalities
>
> Rulers in high places
>
> Stars or morning stars.

All of the spirits were **created** in the beginning.

— Before the beginning, none of them were alive.

— It was God who gave them life.

 READ John 1:3. [2]

God is **greater** than the spirits.

— He lived before them eternally.

— He is the One who made them.

— He gave them life.

God did not give the spirits material bodies when He created them — the spirits do not have flesh and blood as we do.

[2]Be sure to keep on the subject. Don't go into the surrounding context of this verse at this time. ❑

35

— They can move about wherever they want to, since they do not have material bodies.

— But the spirits are **not** everywhere at the same time like God is. The spirits can only be in one place at one time.

— The Bible tells us that even though the spirits do not have material bodies, they sometimes show themselves to people as human beings and may also appear in other forms.

C. The spirits were created to serve God.

 Theme: God is greater than all and more important than all; He is the highest authority.

Why did God create the spirits?

The spirits were all created by God to love and serve Him.

— In the beginning, all of the spirits were God's angels.

— The word "angels" means "messengers" or "servants."

Suggested Visual:

> **GOD'S ANGELS**
> were created to be
> **GOD'S SERVANTS**

— Because God created them, they belonged to Him.

— They were created to do whatever God wanted them to do.

— Illustrate:

What if you take your own kit and make a model car? Who does that car belong to? It belongs to you, doesn't it. What if you draw a picture, using your own paper and markers? It's your picture, isn't it. You are the rightful owner of what you have made.

In the same way everything that God created rightfully belongs to Him. God was the One who made all of the spirits. He gave them life. He made them to serve and obey Him. Therefore, all of the spirits rightfully belong to God.

D. The spirits were created perfect by God.

 Theme: God is holy.

God created all the spirits perfect; not one of them was evil or unkind.

— Everything God does is perfect, because God is holy.

POINT TO THE POSTER, "LEARNING ABOUT GOD." READ, "God is holy...." [3]

— God is holy — everything He thinks, says, and does is **perfect**.

— He never has and never will sin.

E. The spirits were created with great wisdom and strength.

God created the spirits with great wisdom and strength.

 READ Psalm 103:20.

Scripture References (margin):

Genesis 3:24
19:1

Ezekiel 1:5-24

Luke 2:9-14

Psalm 103:20

Hebrews 1:14

Genesis 1:31

Ezekiel 28:15

[3] For this lesson you will only read this part of this attribute.

Theme: God is greater than all and more important than all; He is the highest authority.

— Angels are stronger than we are, and the Bible tells us that God has given them the ability to do amazing things; but they are not all-powerful like God.

— Angels are very intelligent, too, but they are not all-knowing like God is.

God is wiser and stronger than all of the spirits.

— This truth is **very** important to remember.

— No matter what you may have heard or seen presented in movies or books or anywhere else, the Bible tells us that **God is greater than all!** [4]

F. The spirits are innumerable.

 Theme: God is all-powerful.

God created so many spirit beings that it would be impossible for us to count them.

Revelation 5:11 says, *"...the number of them was ten thousand times ten thousand, and thousands of thousands...."*

How could God create so many good, strong, wise spirits?

— He is almighty.

POINT TO THE POSTER, "LEARNING ABOUT GOD". READ, "God is all-powerful. Nothing is too hard for Him to do."

— He can do anything and everything He wants to do!

G. The spirits lived in Heaven.

All of the spirits lived in Heaven with God in the beginning.

— Where is Heaven?

We don't know where it is.

It certainly isn't here on earth!

But it is a real place, mentioned many times in the Bible.

— Heaven is God's special place where He lives.

Though He is everywhere, all the time, Heaven is God's home.

Psalm 11:4 says that *"the LORD'S throne is in heaven."*

The Bible tells us that Heaven is a wonderful place, far better than any place we have ever known or could ever imagine.

H. Lucifer's original position before God in Heaven.

God didn't create all of the angels exactly the same; some were more beautiful, intelligent, and wise than others.

The greatest angel was called Lucifer.

The name Lucifer means "morning star."

God gave Lucifer a very important position in Heaven.

— He was given a place of great authority and power over the other angels.

He, like all of God's creation, was created perfect.

[4] Throughout this lesson, emphasize that God is greater than all. Use the poster to visually reinforce these words. Some of the children may be frightened by the idea of spirit beings. Many may have seen scary movies, etc. Be alert to the children's responses and reinforce the fact of God's sovereignty. He is stronger, greater, than all. By repetition and by teaching God's Word, establish clearly the truth of God's sovereignty. ❑

Ezekiel
28:14

5 The boldfaced part of the verse is what you are teaching here. Do not get sidetracked on the rest of the verse. ❏

— Ezekiel 28:15 says, *"**Thou wast perfect in thy ways from the day that thou wast created**, till iniquity [evil, wickedness] was found in thee."* **5**

I. Lucifer's rebellion

Because Lucifer was created by God and given the highest position over all of the other angels, he should have loved, obeyed, and served God.

But after a time, Lucifer became very proud of his beauty, intelligence, and position.

Ezekiel 28:17

 READ Isaiah 14:13,14. **6**

6 As mentioned in the note in the Teacher Preparation section, be careful to avoid discussion on the surrounding verses, as they will be very confusing and will sidetrack away from the lesson goals and themes. ❏

Lucifer wanted to be like *"the most High."*

— He decided that he wanted to take over God's position as the ruler of all things — Lucifer rebelled against God's authority over him.

— Do you know what "rebel" means?

Suggested Visual:

> **TO REBEL**
> means
> **to think or act against the one in authority —**
> **TO DISOBEY**

— To rebel is very serious.

— Lucifer rebelled against God.

— Lucifer was the first one to do evil. (Evil is anything that is different from what God wants or agrees with.)

You may ask, "If Lucifer was created perfect, how could he rebel?"

— The Bible does not give a clear answer for this, but it does show many examples of the fact that God allows **choices** to be made.

— Look at the passage we just read in Isaiah 14:13,14.

— Note, Lucifer said, *"I **will** ascend," "I **will** exalt," "I **will** sit," "I **will** ascend," "I **will** be like the most High."*

— Lucifer **made a choice** in his mind to rebel against God.

— God could have made the angels like robots who could only do what God told them to do.

— But He didn't. He gave them a choice.

— Consider:

*Think about it: what if someone said they wanted to be your friend — they were willing to do all the things you like to do and they were very nice to you. It would be great to have a friend like that, wouldn't it? It's wonderful to have someone **choose** to be your friend.*

*But what if you found out that the person really had no choice about being nice to you — another person had **forced** him to act that way. That wouldn't be a friendship at all, would it!*

Choice is important to us, and it is important to God, too. He does not program His created beings like robots. He lets them make choices — to obey or to disobey.

J. Other angels followed Lucifer in his rebellion.

Many of God's angels followed Lucifer, their leader. **7**

They joined Lucifer in rebelling against God.

K. God knew what Lucifer and the other spirits were thinking and planning.

Theme: God is everywhere all the time; He knows everything.

Isaiah 14:13,14 says of Lucifer, *"... **thou hast said in thine heart**, I will ascend ... I will exalt ... I will be like the most High."*

God created all of the spirits, and He knew what they were thinking and planning.

— He knew that Lucifer had become proud and wanted to take the place of his Maker.

— God knew Lucifer's thoughts and the thoughts of each of the rebellious spirits.

Nothing can be kept secret from God.

— Nothing can surprise God.

— He knows everything before it ever happens.

— He knows what we are going to think before the thought even comes into our minds.

— He is everywhere.

— He sees everything.

— He knows everything.

L. God removed Lucifer and his followers from their position as God's servants. **8**

Theme: God is holy and righteous. He demands death as the payment for sin.

— Consider:

Do you think God would let Lucifer take His position? What do you think God's reaction was to Lucifer's selfish ambition?

What do you think would happen if someone suddenly tried to take over our government? Our President would not allow it. He would immediately give orders to the military to put down the rebellion.

Our government is important and powerful, but God is more important and powerful than all. He gave life to all of the spirits.

God would not allow Lucifer to take His position.

— No one can take God's place, because

— He is the only true God.

God, in great anger, removed Lucifer from his important position of leadership over the angels.

Scripture References: Matthew 25:41, Luke 8:30, Ephesians 6:12, II Peter 2:4, Hebrews 4:13, Isaiah 14:12-15, Ezekiel 28:16,17, Matthew 25:41, II Peter 2:4, Jude 6

7 This point is a deduction made from several Scriptures, including those listed in the reference column at the left.

If a student questions you on this, you may want to use these Scriptures briefly to support your statements; but be very careful not to get sidetracked. ❏

8 Point L. of this outline must be deduced from several Scriptures, including those listed at the left.

Note the general deductions in the last four statements in Point L.

Again, do not get sidetracked. ❏

God also removed the other angels who followed Lucifer from their place of service in Heaven.

God is holy.

He is perfect and right in everything He thinks and does.

— Anyone who doesn't think and act like God is totally unacceptable to Him and cannot be His friend.

— God would not allow Lucifer and his spirit followers to continue in their former positions in Heaven.

The Bible tells us that after this rebellion they were no longer God's servants; instead, they lived in constant rebellion against God.

We now know Lucifer by other names, such as Satan and the devil.

Satan's followers are called demons.

In the book of Job, the Bible tells us that Satan could still come to speak to God in Heaven.

But Satan and his followers, the demons, could no longer live in Heaven, nor could they be God's servants.

Job
1:6,7;
2:1,2

M. God prepared the Lake of Fire for Lucifer and his spirit followers.

Theme: God is holy and righteous. He demands death as the payment for sin.

God prepared a terrible place of everlasting punishment called the Lake of Fire. [9]

— One day in the future, God is going to send Lucifer, and the other spirits which followed him, to the Lake of Fire to be punished forever.

— God will not tolerate disobedience to Him; God always punishes those who fight against Him.

— Matthew 25:41 speaks of *"everlasting fire, prepared for the devil and his angels."*

— Revelation 20:10 tells us that at the end of the world, the devil will be *"... cast into the lake of fire ... and shall be tormented day and night for ever and ever."*

N. Lucifer and his angels hate God.

Theme: Satan fights against God and His will. Satan is a liar and a deceiver. He hates man.

Lucifer and his followers hate God and every good thing that God loves.

Right from the time when God removed them from His service until today, Lucifer and these other spirits have been fighting against God and everything He does.

Lucifer's name Satan means "enemy, adversary, opponent, or accuser."

Satan is God's great enemy.

— Satan fights against God day and night to try to stop the things God does.

— Satan's demons help Satan in opposing God.

[9] At this point, teach about the Lake of Fire in relationship to Satan only. Don't teach that people are going to the Lake of Fire. Remember, you have not yet taught the creation of man and his sin. ❏

SHOW CHRONOLOGICAL CHART DISPLAYING THE NAMES: SATAN AND HIS DEMONS.

O. Satan and his spirit servants no longer live in Heaven.

Satan and his demons now roam all over the earth.

In the book of Job we read that Satan goes *"to and fro in the earth"* and walks *"up and down in it."*

Job 1:7; 2:2

(Numerous N.T. passages also refer to demon activity on earth.)

P. Conclusion

Theme: God is greater than all and more important than all; He is the highest authority.

Theme: God is holy and righteous. He demands death as the payment for sin.

God is the Most High God and the Creator of everything, seen and unseen.

God is greater than all.

Everything He does is perfect and holy.

He is greater than all created beings:

— God is greater than the angels.

— God is greater than Satan and the demons.

— How important that is for us to know and remember!

God alone can tell us what happened in the beginning.

In our next lesson we will examine what the Bible says about the beginnings of the things we can see:

— The heavens

— The earth.

It's extremely important for us to listen to what He says about creation.

Remember, God was the only One there before the beginning.

QUESTIONS:

---

1. Who is the only One who lived before the beginning? *God.*

2. Where did all the spirits come from? *They were all created by God.*

3. Did God create the spirits with bodies of flesh and bones? *No.*

4. Did God create all of the spirits good, or did He create some good and some bad? *God created them all good.*

5. Why did God create the spirits? *To be His servants.*

6. How many spirits are there? *More than can be numbered.*

7. Where did they all live in the beginning when God first created them? *With God in Heaven.*

8. Who was the most intelligent and beautiful angel created by God? *Lucifer.*

9. What position did God give Lucifer? *Leadership over all the other angels.*

10. What did Lucifer do? *He planned to be like God and to take God's position.*

11. Who else followed Lucifer in His rebellion against God? *Many of God's angels.*

12. Did God know what Lucifer and his followers were planning? *Yes.*

13. What did God do? *He removed Lucifer and the angels who joined him in rebellion from their position as God's servants.*

14. Is there anything that God doesn't see, hear, and know? *No! God sees, hears, and knows everything.*

15. What place did God prepare as a punishment for Lucifer and his angels? *The Lake of Fire.*

16. What is Lucifer's name now and what does it mean? *Satan, which means "enemy, adversary, opponent, or accuser".*

17. Whom is Satan against? *He is against God.*

LESSON 3 — Suggestions for Activities

Be sure to allow time to teach the lesson first!

Listed below are carefully designed activities which will help reinforce and focus on the themes you have taught in the lesson. Choose from this list whatever best suits your students and prepare ahead accordingly. The children may participate in these activities during the time remaining after the lesson has been taught.

1. **Memory Verse — Psalm 90:2**

   Have the children continue to memorize and recite this verse.

2. **Created to Serve / Chose to Rebel**

   Before class, prepare a poster with two columns. Label one column, "Created to Serve," and the other, "Chose to Rebel." Write each phrase shown on the diagram below on individual strips of paper. The children will glue these to the poster during class.

Created to Serve	Chose to Rebel
servant	rebel
obey	my way
privilege	I refuse
worship	won't obey

   Discuss:

   We learned in our lesson that God created all the spirit beings. Why did He create them? (To love and serve Him.) What a privilege that was!

   What was the name of the angel to whom God gave a position of great authority and power over the other angels? Did Lucifer appreciate the privilege that God gave him? Did he want to love and serve God? What did he choose to do instead?

   Notice the two columns on this poster. I have written some words and phrases on word strips. These word strips should be placed under one of the columns. Let's mix up the word strips, and you can each take a turn choosing one. Before you glue down the strip, please read it aloud and tell the class which column it goes in and why.

   Emphasize Satan's rebellion against God.

4. **"I Will"**

   Provide highlighter markers and copies of Isaiah 14:13,14 for each child. (You could type the verses up and copy them on a copying machine, or encourage the children to use their Bibles.)

   Have the children read through Isaiah 14:13,14 and highlight the words, "I will."

   Discuss: "God had given Lucifer the highest position over all of the other angels. He should have loved and served God. But instead, what did he do?"

   Reinforce that Lucifer chose to rebel against God's authority over him.

5. **What's That Name?**

   Before class, write the following names on the board. Leave a blank for the children to fill in the definition of each name.

   1) Lucifer _____ (Morning Star)
   2) Satan _____ (Enemy, Adversary)
   3) Devil _____ (Slanderer)

   Discuss:

   In our lesson we heard each of these names on the board. Do you remember what the name Lucifer meant? Susie, would you write that definition in the blank? This name reminds us that God gave a very important position to this angel. What position did God give him? Did he appreciate the privilege that God gave him? Did he want to love and serve God? What did he choose to do instead?

   Lucifer is now called Satan. What does the name Satan mean? Tony, would you write that definition in the blank? In our lessons we will see how Satan has tried to fight against God all through biblical history. He still tries to fight God. But remember, who is greater than Satan? God is greater than all! He is greater than Satan and all his demons.

   Satan is also known by another name, the devil. "Devil" means "slanderer." Let's write this definition on the board. Does anyone know what slander means? It means to make false accusations against someone else. Who do you think the devil tries to slander? Let's remember again, who is greater than the devil? God is greater than all!

   Strongly reinforce that God is greater than Satan.

6. **Check the Dictionary**

   Provide a dictionary so the children can look up the words "rebel," "rebellion," "rebellious."

   Discuss:

   What does it mean to rebel? It means to oppose or disobey one in authority, right?

   Against whom did Satan rebel? Did God have authority over Satan? Why? (Because God had created him.)

   Emphasize what a terrible thing it was for Satan to rebel against his Creator.

GOD

man

GOD is the greatest! Use the words in the shaded column to finish the sentences below. One word in each block goes with the description of God, the other goes with the description of man.

God had no beginning and will have no end. God is _____.	**dies** **eternal**	Man is born and _____.
God is a _____; He is three persons in One.	**Trinity** **one**	Man is only _____ person.
God needs_____.	**nothing** **many things**	Man needs _____ _____; food, air, water, sleep, light, etc.
God is _____; He does not have a material body.	**body** **spirit**	Man has a material _____.
God is _____, all the time	**one** **everywhere**	Man can only be in _____ place at one time.
God is _____ than all and more important than all; He is the highest authority.	**greater** **authority**	Man should be under God's _____ _____ and listen to everything God says.
God was there _____ the beginning of everything.	**not** **before**	Man was _____ there before the beginning

LESSON 3 Firm FOUNDATIONS **REVIEW SHEET**

skit 3 — God Created the Spirit Beings; Lucifer Rebelled

Readers: Uncle Don, Travis, Jessica

Travis:
That was a scary movie last night.

Jessica:
Mom told you not to watch it.

Travis:
I know. But part of it was exciting. I didn't want to turn it off. Oh, hi, Uncle Don.

Uncle Don:
Hi, kids. What was exciting?

Travis:
Oh, Nothing.

Jessica:
A movie he watched last night. Mom told him not to, but he went back and watched it anyway while Mom was gone for a while.

Uncle Don:
Travis, did you disobey your mom?

Travis:
Yes, I did. I know it was wrong. I wanted to see this movie. Part of it was neat, but part of it was really scary. It was all about these evil spirits and then there were these good spirits.

Uncle Don:
Travis, you really need to obey your mother. You need to go and apologize to her, if you haven't already. And your mother is right — that was **not** a good movie.

Travis:
I've seen other movies like that, Uncle Don. And some of the kids at school see them all the time.

Uncle Don:
Travis, the problem is that movies like that don't show the truth. They are designed to get your attention and make you want to keep watching, but there's nothing good in them — only evil.

Travis:
But are the spirits real? Where did the devil come from?

Jessica:
Travis, you shouldn't ask that!

Uncle Don:
It's all right to ask that, Jessica. As a matter of fact, I was going to suggest that we see what the Bible says in answer to those very questions.

Travis:
The Bible?

Uncle Don:
Yes, the Bible. That's the place to find the truth. Those movies will only put lies into your mind. But God's Word will show you what is true and good. Did you know that the Bible tells us that all the spirit beings, called angels, were originally created by God?

Jessica:
You're kidding!

Uncle Don:
No, in the beginning, God created everything. All of the angels were created by God to be His servants. They were all created **perfect**! God created so many angels that it would be impossible to number them.

Travis:
And all of them were good?

Uncle Don:
All of them were **perfect**. God made the angels very strong. They were created to be His servants and messengers. He gave some of the angels special skills and special jobs to do. The greatest of all the angels was called Lucifer. God put Lucifer in charge of the other angels.

Travis:
Lucifer — isn't he really Satan? Do you mean he was a good angel at one time?

Uncle Don:
That's right. He was created perfect by God. But after a while Lucifer became very proud of his great beauty, intelligence, and his position over the other angels. He decided he wanted to be like God — he wanted to be like the Most High. Lucifer became the very first one to do evil.

Jessica:
That's terrible!

Uncle Don:
Yes, it really was. And some of the other angels followed Lucifer in his rebellion against God.

Travis:
I didn't know this was in the Bible.

Uncle Don:
God did not let Lucifer and his followers get away with their rebellion. God is greater than all.

Jessica:
What did God do?

Uncle Don:
He removed them from their positions of service in Heaven — and He prepared a terrible place of everlasting punishment for them.

Travis:
God really is strong!

GOD'S ANGELS

were created to be

GOD'S SERVANTS

TO REBEL

means

to think or act

against the one in

authority—

TO DISOBEY

lesson

4

God Created the Heavens and the Earth — Part 1

OVERVIEW

This is more than a lesson on the biblical facts of creation. God's nature and attributes are clearly displayed in His creative acts. Your primary goal in teaching on creation is to point out the attributes of God through His creative acts.

Note: This is the first of two lessons on God's creation of the heavens and the earth, followed by a lesson on God's creation of man.

LESSON PREPARATION

This section is for you, the teacher.

The passages in the Scripture Reference column are for your own study in preparing for this lesson. Since they may contain concepts that run ahead of the lesson, they are not to be taught at this point.

Note: If you have not taught previously from this series of lessons, please read carefully the note to teachers in the front of this book.

SCRIPTURE: Genesis 1:1-8

LESSON GOALS:

* To show that God created everything and that He created from nothing.
* To show God's character and attributes as revealed through His creative acts. [1]

THIS LESSON SHOULD HELP THE CHILDREN:

* To give consideration to the biblical account of creation.
* To have an increased awareness of God's sovereignty, His holiness, and His power.

PERSPECTIVE FOR THE TEACHER:

We live in a society that has forgotten its Maker. Theories of evolution are taught as if they were fact; yet the biblical account, given by the One who designed and made everything, is usually totally disregarded.

Unless a person has studied the Bible and drawn his convictions from it, he will almost certainly have been affected by man's incorrect ideas about creation. Virtually everyone in our society has been told by the educational system, television programs, and the print media that evolution is an established fact and that only the naive or uneducated question it. For the most part, evolution is assumed to be fact, not theory. Even little children have been affected to some extent by this teaching.

This lesson will present the true, biblical facts of creation. It should not be a debate of creation versus evolution. Rather, it is a wonderful opportunity to share the truth and to present to the children the fascinating record of creation given to us by the Creator Himself.

Prepare for this lesson by meditating on God's Word. As you teach, share the wonder, awe, and praise that you have for our Creator. Let your students know that you believe God!

RESOURCE MATERIAL:

If you wish to study the evidences for creation, or if you have an older student who asks questions that go beyond the lesson, the following books may be useful:

The Twilight of Evolution, Henry M. Morris, Baker Book House, Grand Rapids, MI, 1963.

MEMORY
VERSE
Hebrews 11:3

[1] Carefully lay the foundations regarding the nature and character of God. For example, you will be teaching that God knew how to create. You will stress that God knows everything about every person. God knows about our sin. God even knows our thoughts. (Note Hebrews 4:13.)

If you don't lay these foundations of truth deeply in the minds of your students now, you are not going to be able to use them later on. The Holy Spirit will not be able to use them to bring conviction of sin.

The doctrine of creation runs throughout the entire Bible, from Genesis to Revelation. Even where creation is not stated in words, it is still an underlying truth — God is sovereign; all things began in Him (Colossians 1:16,17).

Keep in mind however, that most Scriptures which refer to creation also include concepts and truths that have not yet been introduced in your chronological teaching program. The verses used in the outline provide texts that do not jump ahead chronologically. ❏

Job
38-41

Psalms
19:1-4;
24:1, 2;
33:6-9;
95:3-5;
104

Isaiah
40:28;
44:24;
45:7-12;
48:12,13

Jeremiah
10:12,13;
32:17

Colossians
1:16

Hebrews
1:10-12;
11:3

Biblical Cosmology and Modern Science, Henry M. Morris, Baker Book House, Grand Rapids, MI, 1970.

The Collapse of Evolution, Scott M. Huse, Baker Book House, Grand Rapids, MI., 1983.

Evolution: A Theory in Crisis, Michael Denton, Adler and Adler, Bethesda, MD.,1986.

The best source for material presenting scientific evidence for creation is:

Institute for Creation Research
P.O. Box 2667, El Cajon, CA 92021   (Phone: 619-448-0900)

Australian address:

Creation Science Foundation Ltd.
P.O. Box 302, Sunnybank, Qld. 4109, AUSTRALIA

British Address:

Creation Science Foundation
P.O. Box 1427 Sevenhampton, Swindon, Wilts, SN6 7UF, UK

They publish a wide variety of material and will send a catalog on request.

You might even want to set up a time (other than class time) to show a video about the biblical record of creation.

HINTS FOR TEACHING:

Be careful to keep the discussion under control. You are presenting what God says about creation — information which probably has not been previously taught to many of your students. You may find that older students want to discuss evolution. Use discernment as to how much to share in class and how much information you should offer them to read on their own. Try to keep on the subject of what the Bible says. Remember, this lesson is not a debate.

Take your time in teaching. Be sure your students are logically thinking through your points with you. Appeal to their minds and natural logic. Remember, however, I Corinthians 2:14: *"...the natural man receiveth not the things of the Spirit of God: for they are foolishness unto him: neither can he know them, because they are spiritually discerned."* Don't expect them to agree with what you are teaching. Just be sure you are clearly presenting what the Bible says. Expect the Word itself to do the work in their hearts. This may take time. Be gracious with your students, even though they may be wrong and even offensive in their comments. It might be an encouragement for us who teach to remember that some of the most effective and well-known spokesmen for the Word were once outspoken critics of it.

If a student contradicts what you have already taught from God's Word, ask him what God says about that subject. Help him realize that God is the final authority, not you. The issue should be between him and God, not between him and you.

Don't let your students draw you into subjects or details which you should not teach yet. If they ask you a question that will be answered later in the chronological lessons, answer, "That is a very good question. We will find the answer to that question later on as we study further in the Bible."

Don't always correct them if they are wrong.

VISUALS:

- Poster 1, "Learning About God" — You will not be introducing any new attributes of God in this lesson, but use the poster to emphasize the themes as you teach.
- Visual showing the earth's atmosphere

SPECIAL PREPARATION:

- Make copies for your class of the **Lesson 4 Review Sheet** and **Skit 4** (at the end of this lesson). Provide pencils for the children.
- Photocopy **visual** (at end of lesson) — use as small poster or for overhead transparency.
- Prepare for any activity you select from the **Suggestions for Activities** (at the end of this lesson). As you select activities, remember to allow sufficient time to teach the outlined lesson material.
- Bring some pictures of the sky to show as you teach lesson point F.
- Continue to collect pictures for Lesson 5 (See Special Preparation in Lesson 5).

ON TEACHING THIS LESSON:

You are carefully laying a scriptural foundation on which the Gospel will later be presented. Each lesson builds on previous lessons, so be sure to cover each point carefully.

DON'T COMPLICATE THE MESSAGE!

As you teach, keep in mind that this is a directed study — not an exhaustive survey of the Bible. Keep your lesson on track and moving ahead by limiting and directing any discussion.

Carefully follow the outline. Emphasize the doctrinal themes.

LESSON FORMAT: The **center column** below contains the lesson material to be taught to the students. The **bold outline headings** are only for reference and need not be spoken, as they are incorporated into the outlined material that follows. The material in the **side columns** is for the teacher's own reference and is not intended to be included in the lesson.

TO BE TAUGHT TO THE STUDENTS
(Center Column Only)

LESSON OUTLINE:

REVIEW Lesson 3, using the Lesson 4 Review Sheet.

PERFORM Skit 4. Note: "Uncle Don's" part should be read by an adult.

A. Introduction

Have you ever wondered how everything came into existence?

Where did the earth come from?

What was it made out of?

What about all the stars?

What about plants and animals?

What about you and me?

The Bible tells us that **God created everything!**

We are going to study God's record of creation as He has given it to us in the book of Genesis.

Genesis is the very first book in the Bible. [2]

The Bible is a true history — it is God's story of what really happened.

[2] Make sure that the children understand what is a "book" of the Bible. Show them as a class and individually, as needed. ❑

This lesson will cover what God says happened at the very beginning.

— We have already learned that God created the spirits which we cannot see.

— Now we will study God's creation of the universe — the things we **can** see.

B. *"In the beginning God created the heaven and the earth"* **(Genesis 1:1).**

 READ Genesis 1:1.

 Theme: God is greater than all and more important than all; He is the highest authority.

The word "genesis" means "beginnings" or "origins."

— All things had a beginning.

— Nothing/no one (except God) existed before the beginning.

— What then did God use to make the heavens and the earth?

"Created" means "to make out of nothing."

— Discuss:

If a man wants to build a house, what does he need?

If a lady wants to bake a cake, what does she need?

If you want to draw a picture, what do you need?

Can you think of anything you can make without first having materials to use? **3**

3 Give the students a moment to think this over and let it "soak in." ❏

 READ Hebrews 11:3. [Go over this verse several times, having the children say it aloud with you.]

— God made the heavens and the earth out of nothing!

— Only God can make something out of nothing.

 Theme: God is all-powerful.

How was it possible for God to make the heavens and the earth out of nothing?

— The Bible tells us that **nothing** is too hard for God.

Psalm
147:5

Jeremiah
51:15

 READ Jeremiah 32:17.

— God's power is beyond our understanding.

— Is anyone stronger than God?

    Angels?

    Satan?

    Demons?

— No! No one is as strong as God.

— Only God is all-powerful.

 Theme: God is all-knowing.

How did God know how to make the heavens and the earth?

— Compare:

We have to learn how to do all the things that we do.

— We are not born with knowledge and understanding.

— We go to school to learn.

— Many people go on to colleges and universities.

— Some people study all their lives.

— Yet there are still many things men don't know.

But God knows **everything**.

Did God need someone to teach Him?

— Was anyone else living in the beginning who could teach God?

— God did not need someone to teach Him how to make the heavens and the earth.

— God knows and completely understands **everything**. [4]

 READ Romans 11:33.

C. The earth, when first created (Genesis 1:2)

 READ Genesis 1:2.

The earth had no form or shape, and it was completely empty.

— We will see God form it.

— We will see God fill it.

The earth was covered by darkness.

— *Illustrate:*

[Turn off the lights in the room.] *Cover your eyes. Try to imagine what it would be like if there were no light anywhere. Have you ever been in a cave with no lights? It is so dark that you can "feel" it! Imagine this kind of darkness everywhere.*

The earth was covered with water.

— There was no dry land.

— Water covered the entire world.

— There was no life anywhere on earth — no people, no animals, no plants.

Now you may open your eyes. [Turn the lights on.]

D. God was ready to create everything.

 Theme: God is all-powerful.

God is all-powerful, and He was ready to use His mighty power to create.

— The Bible says that the Spirit of God *"moved upon the face of the waters."*

It was **God** who started all things moving!

He is the source, the beginning of all energy.

— God the Father, God the Son, and God the Holy Spirit all took part in the mighty act of creation. [5]

Father—
James
1:17, 18

Son—
Colos-
sians
1:16

*Holy
Spirit—*
Genesis
1:2

[4] You may have students who ask **why** God created the heavens and the earth. Though you do not want to get sidetracked into a discussion like this, you might want to give the student the answer that God does tell us some things in His Word that help to answer that question, and tell them that some of these things will be covered in later lessons.

Use discretion as to how much to share. But it may be a help to the student who is sincerely seeking to know God to see that He truly does have answers in His Word.

Some excellent passages are:

Isaiah 45:18 (God prepared the earth to be inhabited.)

Isaiah 43:7 (He created man to glorify God.)

Psalm 19:1-3 (He created the heavens for His glory.)

Romans 1:20a (All creation shows forth His existence and His character.)

Revelation 4:11 (God did it as an act of His sovereign will [KJV "for thy pleasure"].) ❏

— God is one, yet God is three in one, the Almighty God, the Creator of everything.

— We cannot understand the Trinity; we cannot understand God's mighty power.

E. The first day: Light created (Genesis 1:3-5)

 READ Genesis 1:3.

 Theme: God is all-powerful.

 Theme: God is all-knowing.

Only God could create light by simply speaking!

— Discuss:

Wouldn't it be something if we could simply speak and have light appear? But it doesn't work that way. No, we are totally dependent on light that was created by God from the beginning of time.

What are some of the "lights" we see?

— [Help the children to think of many different kinds of lights, such as flashlights, candles, matches, light bulbs, fluorescent lights, sunshine, moonlight, starlight, etc.]

Whenever we see the light of the sun, the moon, or the stars, flip on a light switch, or light a match or a candle, let's remember that it was God who in the beginning created light. Only God could do that because only God is all-powerful and all-knowing. He created light out of absolutely nothing.

*Scientists can study and describe some of the characteristics of light. All of us are affected by light. But only God **understands** light, for He **created** it.*

 Theme: God is holy.

 READ Genesis 1:4.

The light God made was very good.

— You will notice that each time God created, He said, "It is good."

— Compare:

We are not able to make **anything** perfect.

— Even though things are usable, they still:

Need repair

Wear out

Are replaced because someone made something better.

— What we make can always be improved upon.

— Example:

Have your parents ever bought something to replace what you already have — just because they heard that the new model was better than the old one?

But everything God made was **perfect** because:

God is perfect, holy:

Psalm 18:30; 93:5; 99:3,5,9

Isaiah 6:3

James 1:17

Revelation 4:8

— **God is perfect.**

— God is flawless.

In other words, God is **holy**. [Write the word holy so the children can see it.]

Psalm 18:30 says, *"As for God, his way is perfect...."*

Isaiah 6:3 says, *"...Holy, holy, holy, is the LORD...."*

 READ Genesis 1:5.

God divided the light from the darkness. [6]

— He called the light "day."

— He called the darkness "night."

— This was the first day in the beginning of the world.

F. The second day: Firmament created (Genesis 1:6-8)

 READ Genesis 1:6-8.

On the second day, God created the air and the sky.

— Above this firmament or thin, stretched-out space that we call the atmosphere, God placed some of the water from the world He had created.

Suggested Visual:

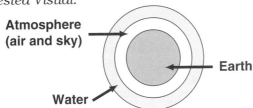

Atmosphere (air and sky)

Earth

Water

— We will see that this water is very important in a later story. [7]

 Theme: God is all-powerful.

 Theme: God is all-knowing.

 Theme: God is holy.

Again God merely spoke, and the firmament was created.

SHOW PICTURES OF THE SKY.

— Discuss:

Think about the the sky — it is so big! We can only see a tiny portion of what encircles the earth. Yet God spoke and created all of the earth's atmosphere, and it was perfect.

G. Conclusion:

Man's ideas of how the world came to be are changing all the time.

But God's true written history of creation has not changed.

— He was there before the beginning.

— He is the Almighty Creator, and He alone knows how all things came to be.

[6] God created light at that time, not the sun. ❑

[7] Although we are not told specifically in Scripture what God actually did when He placed the water above the firmament, many dependable scientists believe that these waters are not the clouds, but water which God turned into mist or vapor and placed as a canopy surrounding the earth, high above the atmosphere. (Reference: *The Genesis Record*, by Henry M. Morris, Baker Book House, Grand Rapids, Michigan, 1990, pages 58, 59.)

It is important to establish that God placed water above the earth so that when you teach the story of the flood, it will be simple to explain how God reversed the process and returned to the earth the water which He had placed above the firmament. ❑

— God has told us throughout His Word that He created everything.

As we study the Bible, we see that God is greater than all, more important than all, and more powerful than all.

Nothing is too hard for Him.

— He is the source of all energy and the Creator of all matter.
— He made everything from nothing.

We have studied the first two days of creation.

We will explore the rest of the creation week in coming lessons.

— As you look at the light and see the sky, think about what we have studied.

— Only God can create, and **He created everything** in the beginning.

— He is greater than we could ever imagine, but He has given us the Bible, His Word, **so we can know Him!**

QUESTIONS:

1. Who, in the beginning, created the heavens and the earth? *God.*

2. **What** did God use to make the heavens and the earth? *God didn't use anything. He made everything out of nothing.*

3. Why was God able to make the heavens and the earth? *God is almighty. There is nothing He cannot do.*

4. **How** did God know how to make the heavens and the earth? *God knows everything and He is all-powerful.*

5. Who taught God how to make everything? *No one taught God.*

6. Is there any person or any angel or spirit who knows everything like God does? *No. Only God knows everything.*

7. What was the condition of the earth before God began to prepare it for people to live in? *It was without form and in total darkness; no land and no life.*

8. What did God **do** in order to create everything? *He spoke and commanded that things appear.*

LESSON 4 — Suggestions for Activities

Be sure to allow time to teach the lesson first!

Listed below are carefully designed activities which will help reinforce and focus on the themes you have taught in the lesson. Choose from this list whatever best suits your students and prepare ahead accordingly. The children may participate in these activities during the time remaining after the lesson has been taught.

1. **Memory Verse — Hebrews 11:3**
   Ahead of class make a poster entitled "God Created Everything — from Nothing!" Underneath, write out Hebrews 11:3 and Genesis 1:1. (You may use this poster with Lesson 5 also.)

2. **Firmament Poster**
   Have the children cut out pictures of the sky from magazines.

   Make individual posters with the sky pictures pasted on colored paper or poster board.

   These "firmament posters" could be used as a background for writing out the memory verse.

3. **Seven Days of Creation**
   Each student could begin to make a "Seven Days of Creation" book for themselves or all could cooperate to make a classroom poster, depicting the "Seven Days of Creation." Pictures could be cut from magazines or drawn and colored by the children.

4. **Model of the Earth** (for younger children)
   Bring "play-dough" and a globe of the earth to class.

   Have each child shape an earth out of "play-dough," using the globe as a model.

   Discuss: When God decided to make the heavens and the earth, did He use "play-dough"? Did He have a big pile of dirt or clay that He used? What did God use to make the earth?

   Reinforce that God is so powerful that He is able to make the heavens and the earth out of nothing.

   Discuss: Did God need a model (like our globe) to show Him how to make the earth? Was there anyone else living in the beginning who could explain to God how to make the earth? How did God know how to make the heavens and the earth?

   Reinforce that God knows everything.

5. **Light and Dark**
   Darken the room — turn out the lights, shut the curtains, etc.

Discuss darkness: What can you see? What would you be able to do if it were always dark? Do you like to be in the dark?

Contrast light and darkness by switching on a light source while it is dark.

Discuss: Can you see now? What are some things you could do now that there is light that you couldn't do when it was dark?

Reinforce how wonderful it is that God created light so that we can see. (You could also discuss other benefits of light to man, constantly reinforcing that this light that God created is helpful to man.)

6. **Light Show**
   Bring a variety of light sources to the classroom, such as a candle, flashlight, lamp, match, lantern, pictures of the sun, etc.

   Discuss: What makes these lights work? (Batteries, electricity, etc.)

   Ask: What did God create light from? What does this show us about God?

   Reinforce how powerful God is to be able to make light from nothing.

7. **Find the Light** (Similar to **Light Show**, but more active))
   Take a field trip inside and outside of your classroom, looking for light sources.

   Discuss: what makes these light sources work? (Batteries, electricity, etc.)

   Ask: What did God create light from?

   Reinforce how powerful God is to be able to make light from nothing.

8. **How Good Was It?**
   Have the children make a poster, "God is Perfect, Holy. The light God made was good, perfect."

   God said that the light was good. Talk about how good it was — not just "okay," but perfect.

   Discuss:

   Can we make anything perfect? (Only God can make things perfect.)

   How can God make things that are perfect? (God is perfect, therefore, everything He does is perfect.)

   "Perfect" means that absolutely nothing is wrong. Everything God does is perfect.

   Discuss: "Perfect" and "holy" are words that describe God. **Everything** about Him is perfect.

Name _____

GOD created the angels

Find the hidden message! Put the answers to the questions in the numbered spaces of the puzzle, using the WORD BANK. Then fill the rest of the blank spaces between the heavy lines to tell how great God is!

WORD BANK

HEAVEN	LAKE OF FIRE	PERFECT	MOST HIGH	ANGELS
GOD	HOLY	SERVANTS	REBELLED	CREATED

1. Who alone was there before the beginning? _____
2. The spirits were not there before the beginning. God _____ them.
3. God created all the spirits to be His _____.
4. Because God is holy, all the spirits He created were _____
5. What is the name of God's special home, where all the spirits lived with God in the beginning?
6. One of the spirits named Lucifer _____ against God.
7. Lucifer wanted to be like the _____ _____.
8. Many of the other _____ also followed Lucifer in his rebellion against God.
9. What is the name of the place where one day, God will cast Lucifer and all his followers?
10. God has never sinned and never will sin. He will not allow those who sin against Him to stay in His presence. God is sinless and perfect. In other words, He is _____.

LESSON 4 FIRM FOUNDATIONS **REVIEW SHEET**

skit 4

God Created the Heavens and the Earth

Readers: Uncle Don, Travis, Jessica

Uncle Don:
Hi, kids!

Jessica and Travis:
Hi, Uncle Don!

Travis:
I'm glad you could come early!

Uncle Don:
Actually, the clock is wrong — I'm a couple of minutes late. The power was off this afternoon for an hour and a half. You kids must have been outside when the lights went off.

Jessica:
You're right. We were out playing.

Uncle Don:
Travis, weren't you planning to finish your science project today?

Travis:
Well, I wanted to, but I haven't gotten all the things I need to finish it. I didn't realize how many materials I'd need.

Uncle Don:
What are you making?

Travis:
Oh, it's just a model of the world.

Uncle Don:
Just a model of the world? That sounds pretty complicated to me. How are you making it?

Travis:
I'm using some clay stuff and wire and . . .

Jessica:
He's really making a mess.

Travis:
She's right, I'm making a mess.

Uncle Don:
You've gotten into a pretty big project, Travis. Do you know how the world really was made?

Travis:
I don't know. Does anybody know for sure?

Uncle Don:
Yes, and we can **all** know for sure, because the One who made it had someone write down how He did it.

Jessica:
Where is it written?

Uncle Don:
It's written in the Bible. God, who created all the spirit beings, also created the earth. He was the only one there in the beginning, and He knew exactly what happened.

Travis:
Well, how did God do it?

Uncle Don:
The Bible says that God **created** the heavens and the earth. He simply **spoke** and there was light.

Travis:
Wait a minute — what did He use to make the earth?

Jessica:
Where did the light come from?

Uncle Don:
The Bible tells us that God made everything from **nothing**.

Travis:
But how could God do that?

Uncle Don:
God is all-powerful; nothing is impossible to Him.

Travis:
But aren't there a lot of people who don't believe that?

Uncle Don:
Yes, Travis, there are. They are some of the same people who can't get their work done when the power goes out and who can't get their jobs done when materials aren't available. But God is never lacking anything. You know, when you were outside, you didn't even know that the power went off. The light there didn't even flicker.

Jessica:
Do any of the scientists believe the Bible?

Uncle Don:
They certainly do, Jessica. The Bible has the only sensible explanation for everything that we see in the world. And God's record of Creation in the Bible never has changed and never will, either. The more that scientists study the Bible, the more they have to realize that every word of the Bible is true.

Travis:
I think my science project is too much for me to handle. Uncle Don, will you teach me more about what the Bible says about Creation?

Uncle Don:
Travis, I'll be glad to! Maybe we can find something for your science project, too. The Bible is the best place of all to learn! 📖

Atmosphere
(air and sky)

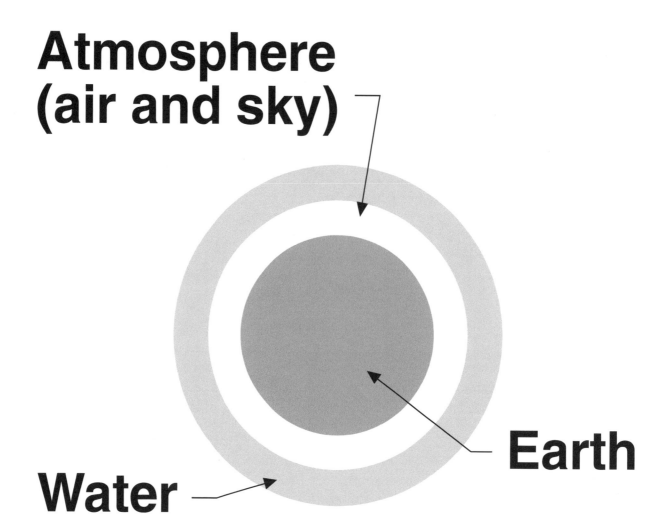

Earth

Water

FIRM FOUNDATIONS

lesson 5

God Created the Heavens and the Earth — Part 2

This is more than a lesson on the biblical facts of creation. God's nature and attributes are clearly displayed in His creative acts. Your primary goal in teaching on creation is to point out the attributes of God through His creative acts.

LESSON PREPARATION
This section is for you, the teacher.

The passages in the Scripture Reference column are for your own study in preparing for this lesson. Since they may contain concepts that run ahead of the lesson, they are not to be taught at this point.

Note: If you have not taught previously from this series of lessons, please read carefully the note to teachers in the front of this book.

Note: This is the second lesson on God's creation of the heavens and the earth. If you are substituting for another teacher and have not yet studied Lesson 4, take the time to thoroughly study that lesson and the preparatory notes and Scriptures before teaching Lesson 5.

Job
38-41

Psalms
19:1-4;
24:1, 2;
33:6-9;
95:3-5;
104

Isaiah
40:28;
44:24;
45:7-12;
48:12,13

Jeremiah
10:12,13;
32:17

Colos-
sians
1:16

Hebrews
1:10-12;
11:3

SCRIPTURE: Genesis 1:9-25

LESSON GOALS:

- To show that God created the heavens and the earth and that He created everything from nothing.
- To show God's character and attributes as revealed through creation.

THIS LESSON SHOULD HELP THE STUDENTS:

- To give consideration to the biblical account of creation.
- To have increased awareness of God's sovereignty, holiness, and power.

MEMORY
VERSE
Genesis 1:1

PERSPECTIVE FOR THE TEACHER:

God's Word is eternal and unchanging. Yet, over the span of a few decades, our society has allowed evolutionary theories to be widely published, taught, and accepted as fact. What is not widely published is the fact that much of the data on which evolutionists once based their theories is now being proven false. Many of the so-called links in the evolution of man have been revealed to be nothing but hoaxes. Other "data" once viewed as evidence for the theory of evolution is being overruled by new scientific discoveries which confirm instead the FACT of creation.

One of the outstanding spokesmen for biblical creationism, Dr. John Whitcomb, has often said that evolutionism is a religion which puts faith in time and chance. All the questions about life and its infinite complexity and order are answered by the evolutionists in terms of millions of years and chance.

Satan has blinded the minds of men, but God's Word is powerful to penetrate that blindness. What good news we can share: God, the sovereign Creator made all things by His power. His Word, the Bible, is the greatest of all texts and the basis for all science. We can teach with confidence — not in time and chance, but in the Living God and His unchanging Word.

REFERENCE MATERIAL:

Lesson 4 lists several kinds of reference materials that may help your students who have questions about creation. Encourage them to use materials like this. Even if you do not have anything available at the time you teach this lesson, you may want to make these resources available to your students whenever possible. Creation is not taught in most schools, so your students may not have been exposed to books that teach it.

VISUALS:

- Poster 1, "LEARNING ABOUT GOD" — Use this poster to emphasize attributes already introduced, and to introduce additional attributes as noted in the instructions in the outline.
- See Special Preparation (below).

SPECIAL PREPARATION:

- Make copies for your class of the **Lesson 5 Review Sheet** and **Skit 5** (at the end of this lesson). Provide pencils for the children.
- For this lesson, **bring pictures of (1) plant life; (2) our solar system, stars, and other things in the heavens; (3) bird and sea life; (4) animals**. Choose pictures with a lot of color and variety. You may want to put these on four separate posters ahead of class time; or you may want the children to help put them on four sections of a bulletin board. How you use the pictures is up to you and your class situation. What is important is to have some pictures to illustrate God's creation. This is especially helpful for children who may not have had much exposure to books and other visual resources.
- For the demonstration given in section B of the lesson outline, you will need some **dried beans and a large pan with sides** to contain the beans as they scatter. Try this demonstration at home until you get a good combination of the right amount of dried beans and the right pan and the right height from which to drop the beans so that they will not just stack up, but scatter across the bottom of the pan. (If you don't have an appropriate pan, you can just let the beans drop on the floor, and pick them up when the demonstration is finished.)
- Bring a **packet of flower seeds**, and, if possible, a flower produced from that kind of seed. (If you cannot bring an actual flower, you may just show the picture of the flower on the packet.)
- (Optional) Try to find some good **microphotographs of plants and plant cells**. These could also be arranged on a poster.
- Prepare for any activity you select from the **Suggestions for Activities** (at the end of this lesson). As you select activities, remember to allow sufficient time to teach the outlined lesson material.

ON TEACHING THIS LESSON:

You are carefully laying a scriptural foundation on which the Gospel will later be presented. Each lesson builds on previous lessons, so be sure to cover each point carefully.

DON'T COMPLICATE THE MESSAGE!

As you teach, keep in mind that this is a directed study — not an exhaustive survey of the Bible. Keep your lesson on track and moving ahead by limiting and directing any discussion.

Carefully follow the outline. Emphasize the doctrinal themes.

LESSON FORMAT: The **center column** below contains the lesson material to be taught to the students. The **bold outline headings** are only for reference and need not be spoken, as they are incorporated into the outlined material that follows. The material in the **side columns** is for the teacher's own reference and is not intended to be included in the lesson.

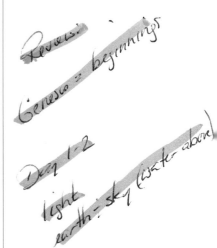

TO BE TAUGHT TO THE STUDENTS
(Center Column Only)

LESSON OUTLINE:

REVIEW Lesson 4, using the Lesson 5 Review Sheet.

PERFORM Skit 5. Note: "Uncle Don's" part should be read by an adult.

A. Introduction

How many of you like homemade cookies?

Just about everyone does!

Well, let's just suppose that your mom made a batch of chocolate chip cookies. Would you like that? Of course you would!

Now let's suppose that you took a bite of one of those cookies, and found that it tasted better than any chocolate chip cookie you'd ever eaten. You might think to yourself, what's in these cookies? They're great!

You might even go and ask how they were made.

Would you ask your friend down the street how the cookies were made? No! Of course not!

Whom would you ask? Your mom!

Why? She was the one who made them.

Think about it: if you want to know about the stars or the ocean, or about flowers or animals or even about yourself, whom do you think you should ask?

Who made everything?

God did, and He wants us to know about what He did, so He has told us in the Bible.

The book of Genesis gives us God's record of creation.

God was the One who created everything.

Only God was there before the beginning, and He knows everything.

In our last lesson, we began to study what the Bible says about God in His mighty acts of creation.

And we read about the first two days of creation.

> We read that God created light just by speaking.

> He created the air and the sky and placed some water above the sky.

Now we will read how God made the land and the seas and filled them with living creatures.

B. The third day: Dry land, ocean, and all flora created (Genesis 1:9-13)

 Theme : God is all-powerful.

 READ Genesis 1:9,10.

God gathered the waters into seas and made the dry ground appear.

— Consider:

Have you ever tried to lift a big bucket of water? Water is heavy, isn't it! Have you ever tried to keep from spilling a glass of water? Have you ever seen the damage done by powerful waves in a storm or by a flood? No man can control the rivers and oceans!

But nothing is too hard for God. Just imagine: God gathered all the waters that covered the whole earth, and He formed the seas and the dry land just as He decided they should be.

 READ Psalm 95:5.

— Only God, who made the waters of the earth, can control them.

 READ Genesis 1:11-13.

 Theme: God is all-powerful.

 Theme: God is all-knowing.

God made all of the plants and trees.

— Only God has the knowledge and power to create plant life.

— God made the plants to produce seeds which would produce more plants just like the originals.

— Consider:

An oak tree doesn't produce pansy seeds! Each plant produces seeds of its own kind.

— Discuss:

What if someone made a nice shirt for you. In time it would wear out, wouldn't it. If you wanted another one just like it, it would have to be made from another piece of cloth and sewn together. But when God created plant life, He put within each plant the capability to produce seeds which could sprout into new plants like the first. So even though a plant dies, it produces seeds that grow into plants like the original — and those plants produce seeds that grow into more plants like the first, and so on. God gives life, and He's the One who keeps it going!

— The plants we have today came from those God created in the beginning.

 Theme: God is love.

— Why did God make flowers, trees, and plants?

   Did God need them?

   No! He doesn't need anything.

   God made the plants and trees for man, whom He was going to create next.

      — God made the plants to meet our physical needs:

         To provide food for us to eat

To give off oxygen for the air we breathe

To provide wood for building

And to provide many other things we need in order to live.

POINT TO THE POSTER, "LEARNING ABOUT GOD." READ, "God is loving...." [1]

[1] For this lesson you will only read this part of this attribute. ❏

— God made the plants to show us His love for us:
He didn't have to make such a variety of colors, sizes, shapes, flavors, and fragrances.
A few kinds would have met our needs.

SHOW PICTURES OF PLANT LIFE.

— Consider:

God could have made everything black and white. But instead, He created colors — beautiful colors!

Everything could have been tasteless. But God created wonderful flavors. (What do you like — chocolate, vanilla, strawberry ...?)

He did the same thing with fragrances.

— He made the earth not just liveable, but truly beautiful.

— He wanted to remind us every day of His great love for us.

— God also wanted us to see that He is a God of order — the **Master Designer** of everything.

— Illustrate:

Think about your favorite kind of flower. Each flower of a certain kind has an identifying pattern that makes it recognizable as that kind of flower — a rose looks like a rose; a daisy looks like a daisy.

SHOW A HANDFUL OF FLOWER SEEDS AND FLOWER (OR PICTURE OF THAT KIND OF FLOWER). GIVE EACH CHILD A SEED TO LOOK AT AND HANDLE.

Each one of these seeds will make a plant just like the plant the seed came from. Look carefully at the seed in your hand. It may look tiny and dry, but it contains all the living information necessary to make a plant which will produce flowers like this, with the same orderly petals and stem and leaves and the same fragrance.

If you were to look at this flower under a magnifying glass, you would see other patterns special to this kind of flower.

If you took a tiny slice of the petal or stem and put it under a microscope, you would see still more orderly arrangements of tiny cells characteristic of this kind of flower.

IF YOU HAVE PREPARED A POSTER OF MICROPHOTOGRAPHS OF PLANT LIFE, SHOW THE POSTER AND EXPLAIN IT.

*All these things show that there is a **Master Designer**.*

— Illustrate:

[Have all the children gather around so they can see what you are doing.] *Let's do an experiment. Let's try dropping a*

I Timothy 6:17b

handful of these dried beans into this pan. Will they make a nice, neat pattern? [Drop a handful of beans into the pan.] No. They scatter everywhere.

What if they did happen to land in some pattern? Would the pattern be the same every time I dropped them? No, it would be different each time, depending on how the beans happened to fall.

*Now, what if I decide to **design** a pattern. I'm going to make a [star] using these dried beans. [Make a star outline, or whatever you wish.] I could do this over and over, because I designed the pattern and can make it again if I want to. This design didn't just happen "by chance;" no, it shows the work of a **designer** — me! I decided what it would look like and made the design.*

*But look at what **God** has designed! **Everything in the universe was designed and created by Him!** He designed and made all the beautiful flowers and plants and everything we see!*

*When you see a **design**, keep in mind that there was also a **designer**. And when you see a design in plants or flowers or any other part of creation, remember that **God is the Designer**. It didn't just happen that way. God designed it all!*

Psalm
19:1-3

Romans
1:20

— Everything that God created on this day was good.

All the plants were good, lovely — created perfect. [2]

— Thorns and weeds did not exist.

— No fruit was poisonous.

— Vegetables and fruit did not get diseases or spoil.

Everything was perfect in the beginning, because God is perfect, and everything He does is perfect.

[2] If a student asks why things are so different now, tell them that in later lessons we will see the answer to that question. ❏

C. The fourth day: Sun, moon, and stars created (Genesis 1:14-19)

We've just looked at a tiny seed; but now let's think about the universe!

The same God who made that tiny seed also made the entire universe — a place so big we cannot even begin to imagine it!

— Illustrate: [3]

The universe is so big that scientists don't even try to measure it in miles; they measure it in "light years." A light year is the distance that a beam of light travels in one year. Did you know that light travels at about 186,000 miles per second? If you could travel at that speed, you could go around the earth more than seven times in one second! But in a year, light travels five trillion eight hundred seventy eight billion miles! [5,878,000,000,000 miles.]

*Did you know that it takes over eight minutes for light from the sun to reach the earth? But it takes several **years** for light from the nearest stars outside our solar system to reach the earth. And we are told that there are literally billions of stars beyond what we can see.*

Genesis
1:31

Psalm
18:30

Psalm
93:5

Psalm
99:3,5,9

Isaiah
6:3

James
1:17

Revelation
4:8

[3] This lesson contains several illustrations which may or may not be appropriate for your class. These are offered as suggestions — use what you think will be understandable and helpful to the children you are teaching. If you choose to use other illustrations, be sure they are carefully researched, as you are using them in context with teaching God's Word. ❏

Now let's read what God says about this.

 READ Genesis 1:14-19.

 Theme: God is all-powerful.

God spoke, and the sun, moon, and stars came into being.

— Only God has the power to create something so incredibly huge!

— In Isaiah 44:24, God says, *"...I am the LORD that maketh all things; that stretcheth forth the heavens alone; that spreadeth abroad the earth by myself."*

— We've already learned how the plants God created show that He is the Master Designer.

— Now we see that the whole universe shows the work of the Master Designer!

Psalm 33:6

Isaiah 40:26

SHOW POSTER OF OUR SOLAR SYSTEM, STARS, ETC.

 Theme: God is everywhere all the time.

We can see only a tiny part of the endless reaches of the universe.

Yet God created even the most remote galaxies and stars — He created everything.

How could God have gotten to all those places that are countless light years apart?

— Jeremiah 23:23,24 says *"Am I a God at hand...and not a God afar off?...Do not I fill heaven and earth?..."*

— Distance is no problem for God.

— God is everywhere.

— We cannot imagine how big the universe is.

— We certainly can't understand the greatness of God!

Although God is present everywhere in the universe, He is the Creator; He is not any of the things He has created. **4**

— The idea that God is everything and everything is God is a lie of Satan.

— There is one true God, not many gods.

— The Bible refers to the universe and everything in it as God's creation, not as part of His being.

 Theme: God is all-knowing.

 READ Jeremiah 10:12.

— God's great wisdom and knowledge are displayed in the universe He created.

— Suggested illustration:

— *As scientists have studied and experimented, they have discovered physical laws, such as the law of gravity. These laws apply here on earth as well as in outer space. Knowing these laws, men have been able to do amazing things, such as travel in space. Yet these laws that men have "discov-*

4 As mentioned before, this is an important distinction. New Age and other pantheistic religions teach that God is everything and everything is God. ❑

Proverbs 3:19

ered" are actually laws that God established and put into effect in the beginning when He created the universe.

 Theme: God never changes.

POINT TO THE POSTER, "LEARNING ABOUT GOD." READ, God "...never changes." [5]

— God never changes, nor do the laws of His creation.

— Consider:

5 For this lesson you will only read this part of this attribute. ❏

Imagine! One system of physical laws controls the behavior of every part we know of the universe! If a car or a space vehicle is going to work properly, it must be built to operate according to these laws. When a spacecraft flies successfully, it is because the men who designed and operated it did everything according to the physical laws established by God.

You don't have to be an engineer or a scientist to see God's laws at work. All of us depend on these laws every day, just to keep our feet on the ground.

Let me see — do you think I can overcome the law of gravity? Maybe if I try hard enough, I can stay up in the air! [Jump up and down and "try" to stay up in the air.] It doesn't work! God's law of gravity brings me back down every time!

Has there ever been a day in your life when the sun didn't rise and set? It may have been hidden by clouds, but it did just what it always does, day after day. How about the moon? Did you know that the movement and position of the moon and earth and sun are completely predictable?

This certainly isn't happening by chance; it was designed that way by God Himself.

 READ Psalm 104:19.

He wanted us to have an orderly world with dependable days, nights, seasons, and tides. [6]

— Compare:

— We get very excited about seeing the launch of one vehicle, such as a space shuttle; and we certainly should, for it has taken an unbelievable amount of research and effort to do all this.

6 If you live in an area where tides are apparent, point out to the children that the tides are completely predictable because God designed them to keep a predictable schedule. ❏

— But imagine God's knowledge! Imagine God's wisdom and skill as a Master Designer! Imagine His power! God spoke, and the entire universe was created!

 READ Psalm 19:1-3.

— We know that God created everything because every day He shows us the things He created.

— Only God could have made the sun and the moon and the stars and the earth and everything in it.

— God has **told us** in His Word, and He has **shown us** in His creation that **He made everything**.

 Theme: God is holy.

Everything God made on the fourth day was good.

— God is perfect, and everything He does is perfect.

— God was very pleased with His creation.

D. The fifth day: All sea life and birds created

 READ Genesis 1:20-23.

 Theme: God is love.

Imagine the beauty that suddenly filled the water and the skies!

— We have already learned that God created a great variety of plant life.

— Now we see that God made many, many kinds of water creatures and birds with countless, colorful designs and shapes.

SHOW PICTURES OF BIRDS AND SEA LIFE.

— The more we search the ocean depths and the remote places of the earth, the more kinds of fish and birds we discover!

— Why did God create such variety and beauty?

He did it to show His love to us.

He did it to show us His power and understanding.

 Theme: God is all-powerful.

God made these wonderful things by His great power and understanding.

— Compare:

Could we make even one little sparrow?

— We might make a model or an imitation.

— But we will never make a living sparrow.

God can; He made the sparrows and every other creature.

— Even the tiniest, most ordinary creatures are God's creation and are incredibly complex.

E. Sixth day: The creation of the animal world

 Theme: God is all-powerful.

 Theme: God is all-knowing.

 READ Genesis 1:24,25.

God created an unbelievable number and variety of animals.

SHOW PICTURES OF ANIMALS

What's your favorite animal? [Give the children opportunity to answer.]

How many of you have a pet?

How many of you to go to the zoo?

Animals are wonderful!

— Consider:

> *Think of all the different kinds of animals and the amazing things they can do! Polar bears swim in the icy ocean; panda bears live high in the mountains and eat bamboo; jaguars and cheetahs can run faster than a man; prairie dogs live in the ground; beavers live in the water and on the land.*

God created each kind of animal with unique characteristics, and each kind of animal is capable of reproducing only other animals like itself.

— Dogs have puppies.

— Cats have kittens, etc.

— Even in the smallest animal we can see that God is the Master Designer.

Only God has the power to create animals.

Man has never created an animal.

Man never will be able to create an animal!

 Theme: God is holy.

All of the living things that God made on the fifth and sixth days were good.

Everything He made was good.

Because God is perfect, everything He made was perfect.

F. Conclusion

God is all-powerful.

He knows everything.

He loves us.

He is the Master Designer.

God made everything out of nothing, and He made it all perfect in the beginning.

Every day, we can look around us and see the things God has made.

Look everywhere and see the evidence of the Master Designer and Creator!

Psalm 18:30; 93:5; 99:3,5,9

Isaiah 6:3

James 1:17

Revelation 4:8

QUESTIONS:

1. Why was God able to command the ocean to go back and stay where He wanted it? *Because He is all-powerful and He created the ocean.*

2. Why did God create everything beautiful, and why did He create water and all different kinds of fruit and vegetables to eat? *He made them because He is loving and kind. He prepared everything on earth for us.*

3. What did God say about all of the things which He created? *God said that they were good.*

4. Why was God able to create all things perfect? *Because He is perfect.*

5. How was God able to create such a huge universe, with so many stars, so far apart? *God is all-powerful and He is everywhere, all the time.*

6. Why did God create the sun to rise and set each day and the moon and the stars to follow the same path every year? *God placed the sun, moon, and stars in the sky to show us the days, the months, the seasons, and the years and to give order to our lives.*

7. Upon what principles do scientists and engineers depend for everything they study and design? *God's laws, which He established when He created the world.*

8. When you see designs and patterns and repeated shapes and orderly arrangements in flowers and trees and all living things, what does that remind you of? *The fact that God is the Master Designer — the Creator of everything.*

LESSON 5 — Suggestions for Activities

Be sure to allow time to teach the lesson first!

Listed below are carefully designed activities which will help reinforce and focus on the themes you have taught in the lesson. Choose from this list whatever best suits your students and prepare ahead accordingly. The children may participate in these activities during the time remaining after the lesson has been taught.

1. **Memory Verse — Genesis 1:1**

   Help the children to learn the memory verse, using the poster from Lesson 4, "God Created Everything — from Nothing!"

2. **Seven Days of Creation**

   Continue to work on the individual books or classroom poster depicting the "Seven Days of Creation."

   Depict the creation of dry land through the creation of the animals (Day 3 through Day 6). Use pictures from magazines, draw, or color.

3. **Flower seeds**

   Bring in a varied selection of flower and/or vegetable seeds as well as dirt and containers in which to plant the seeds.

   Remind the children that when God created the first plants, He made them to produce seeds which would produce more plants like the originals. Each of these seeds will grow into the plant like the one it came from.

   Allow the children to select which plant they would like to grow. Help them plant their seeds. Label the containers well with the name of what is being grown. Watch them grow, week by week.

   Discuss:
   Who created all plant life? How do plants make more plants? How do we know that a marigold seed will grow into a marigold and not into a rose?

   Reinforce God's power to be able to make plants. Emphasize, too, that God is all-knowing. He knew how to make plants, and He knew how to make seeds inside the plants that would produce other plants like the original.

4. **Made for Man**

   Provide art supplies for making posters which show ways plants meet man's physical needs.

   Discuss:
   Did God make banana trees because He needed food to eat?

   Did God make plants because He needed oxygen to breathe?

   Did God make big oak trees because He needed to rest in the shade?

   Did God need to create the plants and the trees for Himself? Why not?

   Reinforce that God doesn't need anything; that He is independent of all things.

   Discuss:
   So if God didn't need to create plants and trees for Himself, why did He create them? (For man)

   Why does man need plants and trees? (Food, oxygen, shelter)

   Make a poster that shows ways plants/trees meet man's physical needs.

   Reinforce God's loving care to create plants in preparation for man.

5. **It's NOT a Boring World**

   Discuss: Have you ever noticed that God did not create a boring world? Can you imagine what the world would be like if God had made everything the same? Just think:

   God could have made everything the same color — maybe ?? (purple).

   He could have made everything the same shape — maybe ?? (round).

   He could have made everything feel the same — maybe like ?? (green slime).

   He could have made everything smell the same — maybe like ?? (fried chicken).

   He even could have made everything taste the same — maybe like ?? (sauerkraut).

   Have the children make posters showing the wide variety that God made — colors, textures, smells, shapes, and tastes.

   Reinforce how loving God is to have created such a beautiful world for us.

6. **Leaf Patterns**

   Collect a variety of leaves. (Either bring them to class, or take the children outside to collect them.)

   Put the leaves under a sheet of white typing paper. Color over the leaves and watch the patterns emerge.

   Reinforce that God is the Master Designer.

7. **Those Amazing Animals**

   Using pictures, discuss the many things animals can do, where they live, their size, special characteristics, etc. The children may like to draw pictures of their favorites.

   Reinforce God's creative power and His understanding. He is the Master Designer.

Name _____

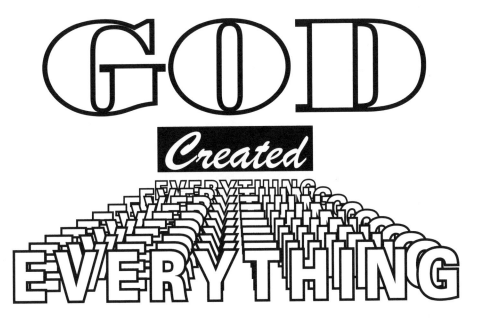

1. Genesis means _____.

2. God created everything out of _____.

3. God could create everything because He is _____.

4. God knows _____.

5. Who was there before the beginning? God the _____, God the _____, and God the _____ _____.

6. On the first day, God _____ and there was light.

7. On the second day, God placed some of the _____ from the world high up

above the sky.

In your Bible, look up Hebrews 11:3. Write the verse on the lines below. When you have memorized it, try to write it from memory on the back of this sheet.

CIRCLE THE
RIGHT ANSWER:

GENESIS is the (last middle first) book of the Bible.

_____

_____

_____

_____

God Created Everything

Readers: Uncle Don, Travis, Jessica

Travis:
Look, Jessica! They're coming up!

Jessica:
What's coming up?

Travis:
The seeds I planted for my latest science project — look at them!

Jessica:
You're right, Travis, they are! How many kinds do you have?

Travis:
Well, there are four: two kinds of vegetables and two kinds of flowers. I couldn't believe all the different kinds of seeds Uncle Don showed me.

Jessica:
Where did you go?

Travis:
We went to the garden shop. They had racks just full of all different kinds!

Jessica:
The thing that gets me is that every one of those little seeds can make a plant. They look all dried up but you put them in the soil and add some water and there comes the plant!

Travis:
I know. I'd never really thought about it until Uncle Don showed us. I really liked all the things he showed us under the magnifying glass, too. Jessica, please hand me that packet of petunia seeds.

Jessica:
Oops! I spilled them. What a mess. They went everywhere. Oh, hi, Uncle Don.

Uncle Don:
It looks like Travis is getting some help on his science project.

Travis:
Jessica is making a mess!

Jessica:
These are hard to pick up. They're so tiny!

Uncle Don:
Tell me, Jessica, did they fall into a nice, neat pattern?

Jessica:
No, they went everywhere. I can't even find most of them.

Uncle Don:
It looks like Travis was able to get some seeds in the right place. Your seedling boxes look nice and neat. Look at this little row of green sprouts!

Travis:
I'm really excited! This was a great idea!

Uncle Don:
Kids, do you realize that all these seeds had their origin from plants that God created in the beginning?

Jessica:
I never thought about that!

Uncle Don:
God is the creator of everything.

Travis:
My science teacher says that everything happened by chance. He says that all the different kinds of things just "evolved" over the years.

Uncle Don:
Travis, did you notice what happened to the seeds Jessica dropped?

Travis:
They went everywhere.

Uncle Don:
How about the seeds you carefully planted?

Travis:
They're right here, in a row.

Uncle Don:
What made the difference?

Travis:
She's messy and I'm neat.

Jessica:
Travis! I didn't mean to drop them. They just happened to fall.

Uncle Don:
You could say that they just fell there by chance, couldn't you. But Travis decided exactly where he would put his seeds, and they are in a nice row. What do you think? Do you think that all the patterns in flowers and trees and leaves and animals happened by chance?

Jessica:
They couldn't! That would be impossible. Somebody had to make them that way!

Uncle Don:
That's exactly right, Jessica. God did. He is the designer of everything.

Travis:
I never knew there was so much to learn in the Bible. And this is just from the first chapter! 📖

lesson

6

God Created Man

FIRM FOUNDATIONS

LESSON PREPARATION

This section is for you, the teacher.

The passages in the Scripture Reference column are for your own study in preparing for this lesson. Since they may contain concepts that run ahead of the lesson, they are not to be taught at this point.

Note: If you have not taught previously from this series of lessons, please read carefully the note to teachers in the front of this book.

SCRIPTURE: Genesis 1:26-31; 2:7

LESSON GOALS:

- To show God's sovereignty.
- To show the uniqueness of man in all of God's creation.
- To show God's original plan for man to be manager over all of the earth.

THIS LESSON SHOULD HELP THE STUDENTS:

- To see man's unique creation (distinct from all the animals) and man's unique relationship to God.
- To see God's ownership of man.

PERSPECTIVE FOR THE TEACHER:

God's Word is very clear in showing forth the uniqueness of man in God's creation. The Bible does not leave an option for man to be any less than **the only being created in the image of God**. This unique creation includes man's unique relationship to God. Man is not only God's creation, made in God's image; man is also God's cherished possession — **accountable** to his Creator.

Believing and understanding this relationship between God, the Creator, and man, the one created in God's image, is essential to understanding all other biblical truth. If this part of the foundation is lacking, nothing else will be stable. The person who is blind to the fact that he was created is also blind to the fact that he is accountable to his Creator. If a person grows up thinking that he evolved, why should he worry about what God has to say?

The subtlety of the lie of evolution is that it deceives man about the existence and character of God and makes man think that he has no need of God. Interestingly, this kind of thinking produces tremendous insecurities because man was never designed to be his own god. We were created to be in submission to One who is almighty, sovereign, all-knowing, all-powerful, eternal; One who can supply **all** our needs. Little wonder that without faith in our almighty Creator, men live lives of utter frustration, for man **cannot** find in himself the supply for all that he needs.[1] The only One who can truly meet our needs is God.

VISUALS:

- Chronological Picture No. 3, Creation
- Chronological Chart
- Poster 1, Learning About God. Use this to emphasize previously introduced themes.
- Visual: God Created Man in the Image of God.
- Visual: God Chose Adam to be Manager over All the Earth.

Psalm
95:6;
100:1-3;
139

Psalm
144:3

Isaiah
45:5-12

Acts
17:24-28

Isaiah
45:5, 21,
22

Isaiah
46:9

Acts
17:28

OVERVIEW

This lesson presents God as the sovereign Creator and owner of man and presents man as God's unique creation, made in the image of God.

Also considered:

"The image of God," with regard to mind, emotions, and will.

Adam, the first and only man created from the ground — the ancestor of all people.

God's choice of Adam as manager of the earth.

MEMORY VERSE
Genesis 1:27

[1] The Bible exalts God as the Creator and owner of man. Humanistic thinking seeks to exalt man as the one in control. Like the lie of evolution, the lie of humanism has permeated our society and deceived many. Even children have been affected by humanistic thinking.

Teach this lesson very positively. You are giving the children the truth. So present it as what it is, a wonderful message! Most children welcome the truth and find security in the fact of God's sovereignty and the uniqueness of God's creation of man. ❏

SPECIAL PREPARATION:

- Make copies for your class of the **Lesson 6 Review Sheet, Skit 6**, and **Review Sheet 6A** (at the end of this lesson). Provide pencils for the children.

- Photocopy visuals (at end of lesson)use as small posters or for overhead transparencies.

- Prepare for any activity you select from the **Suggestions for Activities** (at the end of this lesson). As you select activities, remember to allow sufficient time to teach the outlined lesson material.

ON TEACHING THIS LESSON:

You are carefully laying a scriptural foundation on which the Gospel will later be presented. Each lesson builds on previous lessons, so be sure to cover each point carefully.

DON'T COMPLICATE THE MESSAGE!

As you teach, keep in mind that this is a directed study — not an exhaustive survey of the Bible. Keep your lesson on track and moving ahead by limiting and directing any discussion.

Carefully follow the outline. Emphasize the doctrinal themes.

LESSON FORMAT: The **center column** below contains the lesson material to be taught to the students. The **bold outline headings** are only for reference and need not be spoken, as they are incorporated into the outlined material that follows. The material in the **side columns** is for the teacher's own reference and is not intended to be included in the lesson.

TO BE TAUGHT TO THE STUDENTS
(Center Column Only)

LESSON OUTLINE:

REVIEW Lesson 5, using the Lesson 6 Review Sheet.

PERFORM Skit 6. Note: "Uncle Don's" part should be read by an adult.

A. Introduction

Do you have a favorite story?

Is there a place in that story that you always look forward to hearing — you know, the story builds up to a special part that you can hardly wait to hear?

That part of the story is called the climax.

Of course, not every story is true, and not every story is good. But the story of creation is true and perfect, because it is God's story — the true history of creation!

We have come to the climax of the creation story!

Everything has been building up to this special part.

Just think of what God had already done in the first five days of creation:

— He **spoke** and created the heavens and the earth.

   He created light.

He created the waters above the earth, the expanse in between, the dry land, and the oceans.

He created the plants, the trees, and the flowers.

He created the sun, the moon, and the stars.

He filled the sea with creatures and the air with birds.

He created all the animals.

Suggested Visual:

CHRONOLOGICAL PICTURE NO. 3, "CREATION"

— God had not done all this for Himself; He doesn't need anything!

— Why, then, had God created all these things?

B. The earth finally prepared for man

 Theme: God is greater than all and more important than all; He is the highest authority.

Revelation 4:11

God had done all of this wonderful work of creation because He is greater than all and He chose to do it for His glory.

 Theme: God is loving.

And He did it because He is loving and kind.

God had lovingly, carefully, perfectly created everything in preparation for His final creation: man!

Isaiah 45:18 says that God made the earth *"to be inhabited,"* that is, lived in!

All that man would ever need was waiting and ready.

Compare:

Have you ever watched birds build a nest? The mother and father bird work and work to make a safe, comfortable nest for their babies. They spend hours gathering just the right materials — twigs and grass and sometimes even feathers to make the nest soft and cozy. When the mother bird is ready to lay her eggs, the nest is all ready.

In the same way, God prepared a beautiful, healthy, safe place for man.

C. God's plan to create man in the image of God

 READ Genesis 1:26.

To whom do you think God was speaking when He said, *"...Let us make man in our image..."*? [2]

— It was God the Father, God the Son, and God the Holy Spirit who were talking together.

[2] See notes in Lesson 2 regarding the Trinity, especially the note with point D of Lesson 2. ❏

77

— They were discussing their plan to make man in the image of God.

🔑 **Theme: God is greater than all and more important than all; He is the highest authority.**

God is the highest authority; He is sovereign; He alone decided how all things would be made.

God decided how man would be made, just as He decided how the angels, the sun, moon, stars, the earth, and all things on the earth were to be made.

— Only God decided; He didn't ask anyone's advice.
— God is greater than all and more important than all.
— Man was the most important thing God created on the earth, so God decided to make him in the "image of God."

Job 38-41

D. What does it mean that man was made in the image of God? [3]

What does it mean when God tells us here in His Word that the first man was made in God's image? [4]

— We know it is not talking about our bodies.
  God is Spirit.
  God doesn't have a body of flesh and bones like we do.
— Rather, God was referring to the part which cannot be seen.
  The Bible calls this part of us which cannot be seen our soul and our spirit.
  Man's body was created to be the "house" of this unseen part, the soul and the spirit.

John 4:24

God planned that the unseen part of man would have a **mind, emotions, and a will, created in the image of God.**

Suggested Graphic:

GOD CREATED MAN IN THE IMAGE OF GOD

With a MIND so man could KNOW GOD
With EMOTIONS so man could LOVE GOD
With a WILL so man could CHOOSE TO OBEY GOD

🔑 **Theme: God communicates with man.**

— **Man's mind** — his ability to think:
  Because God has a mind, He planned to make people with a mind which had the ability to know God.

  — God wanted to talk to man, and He wanted man to talk to Him.
  — He wanted to be able to **communicate** with man, not only by spoken word, but also by God's written word, the Bible.
  — God wanted to enable man to do God's work here on earth.
  — Note:
    We realize that God has given animals minds, too. But an animal does not have the same kind of mind that man has. Animals do not have the ability to talk with us; they cannot share our thoughts and make

Psalm 86:11; 119:73

Proverbs 2:1-6

Jeremiah 33:3

John 17:3

Philippians 3:10

I John 3:1, 2

[3] The Bible does not give us a direct answer to this question. The lesson outline covers the answer from a viewpoint of what can be deduced from Scripture.

This discussion is not intended to be the only possible interpretation of "the image of God." ❏

[4] Man was created a rational, moral, and spiritual being, for he was created in the image of God. In other words, man was created so that he could respond to God. He was endowed with intellect so he could know God. He was given emotions so he could love God. He was created with a will so he could choose to obey God.

Make it clear that, when it says man was created in God's image, it was not in the physical image of God. ❏

the kind of decisions we make; they cannot communicate with us by speech and by writing.

God decided that He would give man a mind so man could think and reason like God does.

(Of course, that doesn't mean that any man could ever think and reason exactly as God thinks and reasons.)

— Compare:

Do you know all the things that your parents know? Of course not. But you have a mind like theirs, and they can teach you so you can learn to know the things they know.

Even the wisest man in this world is like a little child compared to God. But because God chose to make man with a mind, he would be able to listen to God's Word, understand it, and then do what God said.

Most importantly, God gave man a **mind** so man could **know God**.

— **Man's emotions** — his feelings:

When we talk about our emotions, we are talking about our feelings — joy, sadness, love, anger, and so on.

— Consider:

People sometimes think that emotions are bad. But emotions are very necessary and helpful. God gave us emotions for our good.

The Bible shows us that God has emotions: He is very kind and loving, but He is also angry at what is evil.

We can see in God that emotions are good.

God loves, hates, feels sadness, and feels joy.

Because God has feelings (emotions), He decided that He would also create man with feelings.

God planned to love man, but God also wanted man to be able to love Him.

God gave man **emotions** so man could **love God**.

— **Man's will** — his ability to choose:

Besides having a mind and feelings, God also has a will; He is able to decide that He will do something or that He will not do it.

Therefore, God decided to make man so that man would be able to make decisions, too.

— Compare:

When you get up in the morning, you or your mom decide what you are going to wear. You decide what you will have to drink and eat for breakfast.

When you get dressed, do your clothes have any say in what you wear? Does your food have any opportunity to say when it will be eaten? No. You are the one who makes the choices about all of these and many other things.

God could have made the first man so he would have had no choice (just like your clothes and your food).

That is how God made the sun, the moon, and the stars. God made them so they have to do the same

A few of countless examples:

Love:
Jeremiah 31:3

John 3:16

I John 4:7-10

Hate:
Proverbs 6:16-19

Malachi 2:16

Sadness:
Matthew 23:37

Luke 19:41

Joy, Delight:
Jeremiah 9:24

Zephaniah 3:17

thing every day, every month, and every year. But God didn't plan to make man like that. God has a will. God decides what He will do, and God wanted man to be able to make choices just as God makes choices.

God planned to make man so he could **choose** to love and obey God.

SHOW AGAIN SUGGESTED GRAPHIC, "GOD CREATED MAN IN THE IMAGE OF GOD."

— Summary:

God gave man a **mind** so man could **know God**.

God gave man **emotions** so man could **love God**.

And God gave man a **will** so man could **choose to obey God**.

— God planned for man to be made in God's image so he could do God's work on earth.

— God was going to give man a special job in His creation.

Man was to be God's special representative on the earth.[5]

God gave man a mind and emotions and a will so that man could do God's work in just the way God wanted it to be done.

That would make both God and man happy!

E. The creation of Adam

🔑 **Theme: God is all-powerful.**

🔑 **Theme: God is greater than all and more important than all; He is the highest authority.**

CHRONOLOGICAL CHART: DISPLAY THE NAMES "ADAM AND EVE."

📖 READ Genesis 1:27, 2:7.

God created the first man and woman. [6]

Where did the first man and woman come from?

The Bible tells us right here. God created them! [Go over Genesis 1:27 several times with the children, until they can say it on their own.]

— **God created** the man first, and then, after the man was living, God made a wife for the man on the same day.

Since the Bible tells us in the next chapter about God's creation of woman, we will wait for a later lesson to read about that.

Today, we will just study what the Bible says about how God made the first man.

— God named the man "Adam," which means "man."

— But after God had made every part of man's body, the man still didn't have life.

His body was not breathing because the part which was to be in God's image was not yet living in his body.

Psalm 97:11, 12

[5] The creation of man was unique. Just as it is important to give God His rightful position, so we should stress the original, unique position which God gave man over creation.

We see our true value and self-worth in the light of God's estimation of us. As a child sees the value God has placed in him, he can better understand the necessity of having a right relationship with God. It is important then for us to emphasize man's unique creation and place of authority on the earth. God placed man as lord or master over the earth to take care of it. ❏

[6] In your attempts to give imaginative descriptions of biblical events, avoid literal terminology or explanations which may give an incorrect picture of God. One man was heard teaching that God put out His hand and picked up the dust to make man. The teacher even asked his listeners if they thought God may have gotten dirt under His fingernails. This type of literalism which presents God as a superhuman must be avoided. Teach just what His Word says, and give it neither a literal nor spiritual meaning beyond what is written. God did not take the dust in His hands to form man. God does not have material hands as we do. God is Spirit. ❏

It was only after God breathed into man's body that he became a living person who could know, love, and obey God.

— Only God could put life into Adam.

Neither the sun, moon, earth, birds, animals, fish, God's angels, any man, Satan, nor his spirit followers can give life.

All things received their life from God and are unable to give life to anything or anyone else.

— Compare:

A light bulb that is not screwed into the socket doesn't give any light. And until the switch is turned on, it still won't give light. When the power goes out, so do the lights! We depend on electrical power for many things we use every day.

Just as the power company is our source of electricity, so also God is our source of life. All things received their life from God and are completely dependent upon Him.

— When God breathed into the first man's nostrils, the man was immediately alive.

He was breathing, and he was a strong, healthy man.

There wasn't any sickness or death in the world.

F. Adam was the first and only man God created from the ground.

 READ Genesis 2:7.

Adam was the first and only man God created from the ground. **7**

God only made one man from the ground and one woman from him, and God told them to have children so all the world would eventually be filled with people.

Adam is the ancestor of **all** people.

— He is the ancestor of all people in every country, of every nationality — people of every race and color and language.

Adam is your ancestor.

Adam is also my ancestor.

He is the ancestor of all people.

We all came from this first man.

G. Man placed as manager over the earth

 Theme: God is greater than all and more important than all; He is the highest authority.

 Theme: God communicates with man.

 READ Genesis 1:28-30.

Scripture References (left margin):

Deuteronomy 30:20

Job 12:10

Acts 17:25

Acts 17:26

7 This is very important. Satan does not want people to know that we all came from one source. We will apply this truth personally again and again as we teach these first 10 chapters of Genesis. It is absolutely necessary that your students come to understand that they, too, had their beginnings "in Adam." They will never be able to understand their salvation "in Christ" unless they understand that they died "in Adam" (Romans 5:12-21; I Corinthians 15:22). ❏

Suggested Graphic:

GOD
Chose Adam
to be
Manager over All the Earth

God put man in charge of the earth and everything in it.

God spoke to Adam and told him what he was to do as God's representative on earth.

Man was to look after God's things here on the earth and to be the leader over the animals, the birds, and the fish.

God had the right to decide to whom He would give the earth.

— He didn't give the earth to His angels.

— He didn't give it to Satan and his demons.

Why was God the only One who had the authority to give man control over the earth and everything in it?

God created everything.

 READ Psalm 24:1.

God owned everything; therefore, He could give it to whom He pleased.

What a special place God gave to man!

By giving man that responsibility, God gave man a great honor.

 READ Psalm 8:3-9. (The teacher or another adult may want to read this passage, as it is quite long. Have the children follow along in their Bibles.)

H. Everything God made was good.

 Theme: God is holy.

READ Genesis 1:31.

Because God is perfect and good, everything He created was absolutely right and beautiful. **8**

— In the beginning, nothing in the animal world would hurt or harm man.

— Neither man nor animal had to kill in order to eat.

— Thorns, thistles, and weeds didn't grow as they do now.

I. Conclusion

God is greater than all; He is the highest authority.

He is the great and only **Creator** of all things; therefore, He is the **owner** of all things.

He made the first man from the dust of the earth.

God created man in His own image, giving man:

— A mind so he could know God

— Emotions so he could love God

8 When you mention God's perfect creation, someone may ask why things are so different now. Don't answer at this point, but tell them that you will be studying the answer to that question in future lessons. ❏

God is perfect, holy:

Psalm 18:30; 93:5; 99:3,5,9

Isaiah 6:3

James 1:17

Revelation 4:8

— A will so he could choose to obey God.

Adam, the first man, is the ancestor of all men everywhere.

As Creator and owner of man, God gave man the responsibility of being manager over the earth.

J. Review

Let's talk about some of the things we have learned about God's creation.

[Give each child a copy of the sheet, "What We Believe About Creation." If you have children who are good readers, ask different ones to read aloud each item. Or, you may prefer to read these yourself as they follow along.

Encourage them to discuss what they believe. Ask them why they believe and encourage them to take this sheet home and put it in a place where they can read it often. Then, when someone asks them what they believe, they will have a clear answer.

Remind them that we are not to argue with people who disagree with us; we are to be very polite. But, whenever possible, we can politely share these truths that we have learned from studying the Bible.

Tell them that we will talk about these things next week, too, and encourage them to study these sheets and the memory verses on their own.]

QUESTIONS:

1. For whom did God prepare the earth? *For man.*

2. What great difference was there between the creation of man and that of the animals? *God created man in His image.*

3. What does it mean that God made man in His image? *God is Spirit, so it was not man's body that was created in God's image. God made Adam and Eve so they could know, love, and obey God.*

4. How many men and women did God make in the beginning? *God created only one man and one woman.*

5. Who is your very first forefather and my first forefather? *Adam.*

6. After the creation of Adam, the first man, over what did God give him control? *The earth and everything in it.*

7. Why don't Satan and his demons have the right to control the earth and the things on the earth? *Because God never gave them the right to control anything on the earth. God gave the earth to man.*

8. What was everything in the world like in the beginning? *Very good. Everything was perfect.*

LESSON 6 — Suggestions for Activities

Be sure to allow time to teach the lesson first!

Listed below are carefully designed activities which will help reinforce and focus on the themes you have taught in the lesson. Choose from this list whatever best suits your students and prepare ahead accordingly. The children may participate in these activities during the time remaining after the lesson has been taught.

1. Memory Verse — Genesis 1:27

Write the verse on the board, say it together, then erase a word and say the verse again from memory. Continue to do this, erasing a word after each time the verse is repeated.

2. Seven Days of Creation

Continue to work on the individual books or classroom poster depicting the "Seven Days of Creation."

Depict the creation of Adam. Use pictures from magazines, draw, or color.

3 This Wonderful Body

Make the children aware of the wonderful way God created our bodies.

Discuss:

Have you ever thought about the wonderful way our bodies work? Unless we are sick, our bodies usually work so efficiently and automatically that we don't even realize how amazing they are.

Look at this (show a picture or have them look at a person). What do you see? How did your body process that information? (Eye sent images to the brain.)

Stand up and try to walk without using your big toe. Our toes give balance when we walk.

Sit perfectly still and notice what your body is doing. What are you doing? (Breathing, blinking, heart is pumping.) Do you even have to think about those things? Isn't that amazing!

Does anybody know how your lungs work? What about your heart?

Look at your skin. It is flexible, waterproof, etc. If you tear your shirt, will it repair itself? Of course not! But what if you get a scratch or a cut on your hand or knee? Does the wound stay open the rest of your life? No! It will heal over.

Aren't these wonderful bodies that God has given us!

Reinforce God's power in creating our amazing bodies. Reinforce also that God is the Master Designer.

4. Think It Through

Give children a few fun riddles to think through. Discuss:

Why can you think things through? (Because God created people with the ability to think, to learn.)

Why did God create people with minds? (So they would be able to know God.)

How can you use your mind to know more about God? (Read the Bible, listen in class.)

Reinforce that God created man with a mind because He wanted us to be able to know Him.

5. Ancestors — Descendants

Have the children make a poster showing relationships and defining the words, "ancestor" and "descendant." The poster might look like this:

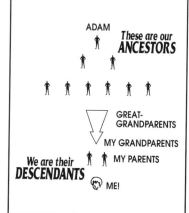

6. Choices

Have a discussion with the children about choices they make. You could confine the discussion to choices made that day, or that week, or just keep it general.

Ask "What choices have you made today?" (Below are sample ideas if you need to prompt them). Write their responses on the blackboard.

— to get out of bed when Mom woke me up

— to eat cereal instead of toast for breakfast

— to wear blue pants instead of brown pants

— to listen in class

Discuss:

Where did your ability to make choices come from?

Are you glad God made man with the ability to make choices? Why?

What would life be like for you if you could not make choices?

Reinforce that God chose to make man with a will so that man would choose to love and obey God.

Caution: Avoid pushing the children to make a decision to love and obey God. Remember that obedience to God apart from Jesus Christ will prove impossible.

God created everything

DESIGNER

CREATOR

God designed everything

This picture shows many things which God created and designed. List the things you can find!

_____

_____

_____

_____

_____

_____

_____

Use this WORD BANK to fill in the answers to the questions below:

God   spoke   God   loves   designer   good

1. God created many variety of plants and trees and flowers because He _____ us.

2. To create the sun, the moon, and all the stars, God just _____.

3. All of the laws that control the universe were originally established by _____.

4. Can anyone besides God make a living creature?   YES   NO

5. God said that everything He created was _____.

6. Whenever you see a design, you know that there had to be a _____.

7. Who designed everything in the universe? _____

Have you learned Hebrews 11:3? Try to write it out from memory. Look in your Bible to see if you are correct. When you have this verse memorized, write it again on the back of this paper.

_____

_____

_____

_____

_____

Name _____

What We Believe About Creation

1. **We believe that God created everything because we believe the Bible.** The Bible tells us clearly that God created everything. The Bible is not just a religious book. It is a book of facts — a history book authored by God. Many details of the Bible, even back to Genesis, are being shown true as archeologists dig up the remains of ancient civilizations. Names, dates, and places agree with what is in the Bible.

2. **God is the author of the Bible.** Even though He used over 40 men and took about 1,600 years to write it, the Bible reads like a book written by one author. It has unity because God is the author of all of the Bible. He told men exactly what to say.

3. **God was the only one there before the beginning.** Only He knows what happened in the beginning. In the Bible He tells us what happened.

4. **Things did not just happen "by chance;" everything was created by God, according to His plan.** Look at the very tiny things we see through a microscope, and then look at the huge things like the solar systems and galaxies. They have a design, because they were made by a designer. If things just exploded or fell where they were, things would not have patterns like we see. The patterns in the things God has made are beautiful and are repeated over and over, but each design is just a little different. Snowflakes, for example, are all basically six-sided patterns, but each snowflake is different from all the others!

   When we see a design, we know there has to be a designer. And when we see designs in the world around us, we know that the Designer and Creator is God!

5. **God's laws that control the physical universe have not changed.** Men have learned many of God's laws, such as the law of gravity. But these laws were established by God in the very beginning. When men are able to achieve great things, such as sending up a space craft, they are using the laws which God established. Men are continually writing new books because they are learning new things and the old books become outdated. But God's laws that control the physical universe have never changed.

6. **Animals and plants always produce more animals and plants after their kind.** Cats have kittens; dogs have puppies. Even a tiny petunia seed will grow to make a petunia, and it will make **only** a petunia. God tells us in Genesis 1 that He made the plants and animals to reproduce after their own kind.

7. **No one but God is able to create all that was created.** Only God is strong enough, wise enough, and able to be everywhere all the time. Only God can make something from nothing.

   HEBREWS 11:3 IS OUR MEMORY VERSE ABOUT GOD'S CREATION!

GOD CREATED EVERYTHING

skit 6   God Created Man

Readers: Uncle Don, Travis, Jessica

Uncle Don:
Hi, Jessica. It's good to see your dad home from his business trip.

Jessica:
I'm glad he's home. We miss him when he's gone so much.

Uncle Don:
Well, he misses you, too. Where's Travis?

Jessica:
Oh, he's over in the garage talking to dad about that wooden chest he found in the moving stuff.

Uncle Don:
Travis sure wanted that! He was trying to convince himself that it was just some moving box. But I know that your dad made that himself. I don't remember all the details, but I think it has a special purpose.

Jessica:
Here comes Travis now.

Uncle Don:
Hi, Travis. How are you today?

Travis:
Fine, thanks. Uncle Don, I'm sure glad I listened to you and waited for dad before I took that wooden chest and put my model stuff in it!

Uncle Don:
Well, I knew that your dad had made it himself, and I think it has some special purpose.

Travis:
He did make it! I couldn't believe it! It's really neat. He said he doesn't have time to do that kind of work now that he travels so much.

Jessica:
So what's it for, anyway?

Travis:
It holds all of his antique woodworking tools. He said he's had them packed away for years. When we moved he decided that he was going to put them out on display in that case again. He made the case when he and mom were first married.

Jessica:
It's beautiful! Where did he get the tools?

Travis:
They belonged to his great grandfather. Every space in that case holds one of those tools just perfectly!

Jessica:
I'm glad you didn't put your models in it!

Travis:
Me, too! Dad said he might make me a case someday — just special for my models. I'd sure like that!

Uncle Don:
There's a good lesson in that wooden case.

Jessica:
What do you mean?

Uncle Don:
Well, your dad made that case. He owned it, and it was his to do with as he pleased because he made it. He designed it for a special purpose. Did you ever stop to think that God made man?

Jessica:
Made man? Out of what?

Uncle Don:
The Bible tells us that God made man out of the dust of the ground.

Travis:
Dust? Our science book says man just evolved.

Uncle Don:
The Bible tells us that God made the first man out of the dust. And it was God who breathed life into man. God is the Creator of man, the owner of man. Man belongs to God. God is the one who knows what man is made for, and the one who knows what is best for man.

Jessica:
I never thought about that!

Uncle Don:
Most people don't. But it's very important. Your dad made that wooden case, therefore it belonged to him. He made it. It was up to him what should be done with it.

Travis:
And here I was trying to believe that it was just a moving box and I could do whatever I wanted with it!

Uncle Don:
Travis, that's kind of like the way people think when they refuse to believe that God created them.

Travis:
What do you mean?

Uncle Don:
People who think that man evolved don't realize that God is the Creator and owner of man. They think they can do whatever they want.

Travis:
Just like I almost did with the case!

GOD CREATED MAN

IN THE IMAGE OF GOD

With a MIND so man could
KNOW GOD

With EMOTIONS so man could
LOVE GOD

With a WILL so man could
CHOOSE TO OBEY GOD.

GOD

Chose Adam

to be

Manager over All

the Earth.

lesson

7

FIRM FOUNDATIONS

God Placed Adam in Eden

OVERVIEW

This lesson continues to present God's sovereignty as Creator and owner of man. It also establishes the fact tht the penalty for sin is death.

Also presented:

— God's rest on the 7th day: not a physical rest, but a ceasing from work that was completed

— God's placing Adam in the garden: an act of God's sovereignty as the creator/owner of man

— God's care for Adam

— The Tree of life: God wanted Adam to choose to eat of it and live forever

— The tree of knowledge of good and evil: God instructed Adam clearly that he would die if he disobeyed God and ate of this tree

— Death penalty for sin: separation from God, separation from the body, separation forever in the Lake of Fire.

LESSON PREPARATION

This section is for you, the teacher.

The passages in the Scripture Reference column are for your own study in preparing for this lesson. Since they may contain concepts that run ahead of the lesson, they are not to be taught at this point.

Note: If you have not taught previously from this series of lessons, please read carefully the note to teachers in the front of this book.

SCRIPTURE: Genesis 2:1-9,16,17

LESSON GOALS:

- To present God as the sovereign, loving, wise Creator and owner of man.
- To establish that the penalty for sin is death.

THIS LESSON SHOULD HELP THE STUDENTS:

- To see their need to get to know God.
- To see their need to be in submission to God.
- To value God's care for them.
- To see that the penalty for sin is death.

PERSPECTIVE FOR THE TEACHER:

This is a lesson about God's sovereignty and holiness and man's relationship to his God. Our society teaches us to be independent and to do "our own thing"; God's Word teaches us to be in complete submission to our holy, righteous Creator. Our society teaches us to stand up for our rights; the Bible teaches us the privilege of receiving what is given to us by our sovereign, loving, all-knowing God. Our society teaches us to go as far as we dare and to get away with whatever we can; God's Word teaches us that God is holy and that the punishment for sin is death. Our society tells us to find out who we are so that we can have more self-esteem; God's Word says we should first know Him and then understand who we are in Him!

The Bible tells us that the fear of God *"is the beginning of knowledge"* (Proverbs 1:7). Contrary to popular opinion, the truths in this lesson will give stability and strength to the children. God is to be trusted — He is firm in His holiness. Knowing this makes His grace seem even more marvelous in our eyes!

SPECIAL NOTE:

This lesson presents some concepts which are seldom taught in our culture: God's ownership of man and man's need to fear God. To prepare your own heart for teaching and for handling any discussion on these issues, be sure to study ahead the Scriptures in the side columns adjacent to the lesson outline.

MEMORY
VERSE
Psalm 24:1, 2

VISUALS:

- Poster 3, "The Penalty for Sin Is Death"
- Poster 1, "Learning About God" — Use this poster to emphasize previously introduced themes and to introduce new attributes of God.
- A tree branch with green leaves (see Special Preparation)

SPECIAL PREPARATION:

- Bring a tree branch with green leaves (or needles). You will use this branch in several future lessons to illustrate the effect of sin in separating man from God, man's source of life. A small branch is all that's needed; you will want something small enough that you can conveniently store it between lessons.
- Make copies for your class of the **Lesson 7 Review Sheet** and **Skit 7** (at the end of this lesson). Provide pencils for the children.
- Prepare for any activity you select from the **Suggestions for Activities** (at the end of this lesson). As you select activities, remember to allow sufficient time to teach the outlined lesson material.

ON TEACHING THIS LESSON:

You are carefully laying a scriptural foundation on which the Gospel will later be presented. Each lesson builds on previous lessons, so be sure to cover each point carefully.

DON'T COMPLICATE THE MESSAGE!

As you teach, keep in mind that this is a directed study — not an exhaustive survey of the Bible. Keep your lesson on track and moving ahead by limiting and directing any discussion.

Carefully follow the outline. Emphasize the doctrinal themes.

LESSON FORMAT: The **center column** below contains the lesson material to be taught to the students. The **bold outline headings** are only for reference and need not be spoken, as they are incorporated into the outlined material that follows. The material in the **side columns** is for the teacher's own reference and is not intended to be included in the lesson.

TO BE TAUGHT TO THE STUDENTS
(Center Column Only)

LESSON OUTLINE:

REVIEW Lesson 6, using the Lesson 7 Review Sheet.

PERFORM Skit 7. Note: Uncle Don's part should be read by an adult.

A. Introduction

Have you ever started something and not finished it?

All of us have!

— Can you think of something you started recently and didn't finish?

Why didn't you finish what you started? [1]

— You changed your mind.

— You lost interest.

[1] Give your students a brief opportunity to name some of their reasons for not finishing what they started. ❑

— It turned out to be too hard for you to do.

— It was a bigger job than you had thought.

— You were interrupted.

— You ran out of time.

— Etc.

God is not like us.

— He never gives up on what He plans to do.

— When He starts to do something, He **always** finishes it.

B. God finished making all He had planned.

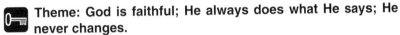 **Theme: God is greater than all and more important than all; He is the highest authority.**

Theme: God is faithful; He always does what He says; He never changes.

READ Genesis 2:1.

God finished all that He planned to do.

— Compare:

    We change our minds and we change our plans.

    But it is never that way with God.

God never changes His mind about anything that He plans.

POINT TO THE POSTER, "LEARNING ABOUT GOD." READ, "God is faithful; He always does what He says; He never changes."

Nothing and no one can keep God from doing all He plans to do.

— No human can stop God.

— Satan cannot stop God.

— God is greater than all.

He always does whatever He plans to do.

Therefore, when God promises to do something, we can be absolutely certain that He will do it.

C. God rested from His work of creation on the seventh day.

 Theme: God is all-powerful.

 READ Genesis 2:2,3.

How many days did it take for God to make everything? Only six days! **2**

— Compare:

Have you ever watched as a house was being built? It takes a long time, doesn't it?

But look at all the things God created in just six days. There is no one as great as God. He is almighty. He can do anything He wants.

Scripture References (margin):
Psalm 33:11; 115:3; 135:5, 6

Isaiah 46:10, 11; 55:8-11

Teacher's Notes (margin):
2 A student may ask if these are six 24-hour days.

(Don't raise this point unnecessarily.)

Probably the clearest answer we have from Scripture is the words, *"the evening and the morning were the first [second, third, fourth, etc.] day"* (Genesis 1:5, 8, 13, 19, 23, 31). This would indicate 24-hour days.

Many people view these days as ages of time in which everything evolved.

But nowhere in the Bible does God say anything like this. II Peter 3:8 says that *"one day is with the Lord as a thousand years,"* but the context is very different from the Genesis 1 context which mentions morning and evening and a clear succession of numbered days. ❑

93

3 Someone may raise the question of sabbath days or going to church on Sunday. Avoid this discussion at this point.

You might want to say that in this lesson we are just going to focus on what God is saying about His rest from creating all things. ❏

God finished in six days all He planned to do, so on the seventh day, He rested from His work of creating. **3**

— Did God rest from His work because He became tired after all the work He had done?

— Compare:

After playing hard all afternoon, you want to come in and rest, don't you! What about your dad when he mows the lawn, or your mom when she has cleaned the house and done all the laundry. They are tired, aren't they? And they are glad for a rest. But just think of all that God had done that week!

Do you think that God rested because He was tired? He had made millions of stars, the sun, and the moon. Look at all the things He created on the earth. Do you think He lay down and said, I'm tired. I am going to have a good rest today?

No, God doesn't get tired or sleepy like we do. He doesn't have a physical body that needs rest or sleep. God is Spirit. He is always the same. He is still the same today as He was when He first made the earth. God will never change.

 READ Isaiah 40:28.

No, God wasn't tired — He rested because He **finished** everything He had planned to do!

— Compare:

What if you built a model airplane and finally finished it. You might just step back and take a good look at it and admire the completed job. Even if you had the energy to do more, you wouldn't, because everything that needed to be done was finished.

That's how it was with God and all He had created. He had done all He planned to do, and He was very pleased with everything that He had made.

God created everything in six days, and so He rested on the seventh day.

He rested from creating because He saw that all His work which He had planned to do was finished.

D. Mist, not rain, watered the earth.

 READ Genesis 2:4-6.

These verses teach us something very interesting about the beginning.

— When God first created everything, He did not water the earth by giving rain.

— Instead, He watered it by mist which came up from the earth. **4**

E. God planted a garden.

 Theme: God is love.

 READ Genesis 2:7,8.

Because God loved Adam very much, God planted a beautiful garden especially for Adam. **5**

God included in that garden all the vegetables and fruit trees that Adam needed to keep him healthy, strong, and happy.

— Compare:

Have you ever made something special for your mom or dad — just because you love them?

God planted a beautiful garden for Adam — because God loved him!

All of the gardens and zoos in the world could not begin to compare with God's garden and all the wonderful animals He created.

F. God put Adam in the garden.

 Theme: God is greater than all and more important than all; He is the highest authority.

 READ Genesis 2:8.

When God had the garden ready, He took Adam and put him there.

— God didn't ask Adam if he wanted to live there.

— God just took Adam and put him in the garden called Eden. **6**

— Why could God do this?

— Because God **created** man, He had the right to put him where He wanted him and to tell him what to do.

— Illustrate:

*In some areas of the world, the idea of the maker and the owner of things is easily understood, because people have to make for themselves **everything** they use.*

For example, if a man said, "Who owns that canoe?" the answer would be the name of whoever made it. He made it; therefore, he owns it, and it's his to do with as he wants.

If you sat down at home and used your materials and took time to draw a special picture, would you let anybody take that picture and do whatever they wanted with it? No, you were the one who made it, and you'd want to decide what should be done with it.

Who owned Adam? God did, because God created Adam, and God had the right to put Adam where God wanted him to be.

— God is the owner of all things.

He has the right to do what He wishes with us and with all the other things that He has made.

He has the right to tell us what to do.

God **created** Adam, so Adam **belonged** to God.

 Theme: God is love.

 Theme: God is holy and righteous.

5 Note to substitute teacher: The creation of man was covered in Lesson 6. ❏

6 Some students may ask where the Garden of Eden was located. Bible scholars take different views about this. Some believe it was located in the area of present-day Iraq, as the rivers there bear the same ancient names given in Genesis 2.

Others believe that those who survived the flood of Genesis 6 and 7 gave these pre-flood names to new rivers in a landscape totally transformed by the destructive deluge. They believe that the location of the Garden of Eden is impossible to ascertain. (See *The Genesis Record*, by Henry Morris, p. 90.) ❏

I Chronicles 29:11,12

Psalm 24:1; 97:9; 100:3

Jeremiah 10:10, 23

Theme: God never changes.

God told Adam to take care of the garden, but Adam didn't need to work hard because everything was perfect.

— The weeds didn't grow.

— Snails, grubs, and insects did not eat the fruit or vegetables.

— Consider:

> *Everything was beautiful and perfect!*
>
> *What happened? Why are things so different now? The Bible tells us exactly what happened to change everything, and we will study that part later on.*

G. The tree of life and the tree of the knowledge of good and evil

 Theme: Man needs God.

 READ Genesis 2:9.

God planted two very important trees in the middle of the garden: the tree of life and the tree of the knowledge of good and evil.

God was Adam's source of life.

— God wanted Adam to have what was good.

— Adam was dependent upon God for everything; God made Adam and everything else in all creation.

 READ Genesis 2:16,17.

 Theme: God communicates with man.

God told Adam what was good to do and what was not good to do:

— When God put Adam in the garden, God did not leave it up to Adam to decide what was right and what was wrong.

— God spoke to Adam and told him what he must not do and what would happen if he disobeyed.

— Compare:

> *Have you ever had your dad or mom or your teacher tell you what was right to do and what was wrong? Of course you have! And it was for your own good. When you were little, your parents taught you not to cross the street without looking both ways. They taught you not to touch the hot stove. Why would they do that? Because they love you, and because you needed to have them tell you — you wouldn't have made good choices on your own.*

God clearly instructs us, too:

— He hasn't changed.

— He has not left us to decide for ourselves what is right and what is wrong.

— God has given the Bible so we can know what pleases and displeases Him.

God instructed Adam:

— God planted an endless variety of trees — trees which supplied food for man and gave beauty to the garden.

— Only **one** tree was a no, no for Adam.

— He must not eat of the fruit from this tree which was called the tree of the knowledge of good and evil.

God knew what was best for Adam.

— From the time God created Adam, God had decided what was good for him.

— Adam didn't know anything that was evil or bad because God had given him everything that was good.

Adam could choose to obey or to disobey God.

— Adam could choose to obey God and eat only what God had said was good.

— He could eat of the tree of life and live forever.

— But if Adam disobeyed God and ate the fruit from the tree of the knowledge of good and evil, it would be because Adam had decided that he wanted to be independent of God.

— [Being independent means to do our own thing — to refuse to obey those in authority over us.]

— From the time he ate, he would not only know what was good but he would also know what was evil.

— Instead of God telling him what was good and what was evil, he would have to choose for himself.

If Adam disobeyed God and wanted to be independent of God, then the result would be death, separation from God.

**Deuter-
onomy
30:19, 20**

**Romans
6:23a**

H. Death is the punishment for disobedience to God.

 Theme: God is holy and righteous. He demands death as the payment for sin.

READ Genesis 2:17.

God warned Adam: If you eat the fruit of this tree, you will die immediately.

What did God mean when He told Adam that he would die?

SHOW POSTER, "THE PENALTY FOR SIN IS DEATH." REFER TO THIS POSTER AS YOU GO THROUGH THE FOLLOWING EXPLANATION.

1. Separation from God — death of man's relationship with God.

— Adam would be immediately separated from God.

— Compare:

Do you remember what happened to Satan and the angels when they rebelled against God?

They were cut off from God's love and friendship.

— *They were separated from God.*

— *They were put out of their positions in Heaven, and God prepared a place of terrible punishment where He is going to put them forever.*

**Isaiah
14:13-15**

**Ezekiel
28:14-17**

**II Peter
2:4**

Jude 6

**Revela-
tion
20:10**

— Compare:

Sometimes grownups get into big arguments with one another. They disagree on something important and then they just quit spending time together. They don't want to do things together any more. They are no longer friends because a major disagreement has separated them.

— God warned Adam that, if he disobeyed His command, he would no longer be God's friend.

Adam would become God's enemy as Satan had.

Adam would be separated from God's love and friendship.

Adam would die.

Adam would be separated from God, the source of life and all that is good.

That part of Adam which was created in God's image so Adam could know, love, and obey God would be separated from God if Adam ate the forbidden fruit.

2. **Separation from the body** — death of man's physical body.

— God didn't mean that Adam would die physically the same day he ate the fruit.

— God meant that on that day, Adam would be cut off from God who was the source of his life.

— Because of this, he would also have to die physically.

DISPLAY BRANCH BROKEN OFF FROM A TREE

— Discuss:

What happens when a branch is cut off from a tree? The branch doesn't die immediately, does it? The leaves (or needles) are still green for a few days, and it looks just like it did before it was cut. But because it has been separated from the tree, it cannot receive what it needs to keep it alive. It has been cut off from its source of life. Very soon, it will dry up.

That's what God meant would happen to Adam. If Adam ate of this fruit, he would be immediately cut off from God, the source of his life.

— Explain:

When a person dies, he is separated from his body. A person's spirit and soul, that is, the parts of him which cannot be seen, leave his body and so he dies.

When God first created Adam's body, Adam didn't have any life. His body was like a dead person's body. Then God breathed life into Adam's nostrils. When God breathed into Adam's body, God gave him his soul and spirit. Our bodies are the houses of our souls and spirits.

— Compare:

When you go to visit your neighbors, you go to their house. But if they have moved away to another town, they have left their house and are no longer living in it. They are separated from the place where they used to live. If someone asks where they are living, you would say, "They have moved away to another town. They are not living here anymore."

That is what happens when a person dies. He leaves his body.

— If Adam disobeyed God, Adam's body would eventually die.

3. Separation forever in the Lake of Fire — death to any enjoyment of God and His blessings.

— Finally, if Adam disobeyed God, then not only would his body die, but he would also go eventually to the Lake of Fire.

— This is the same place of terrible punishment which God prepared for Satan and his spirit followers.

— Adam's punishment would be forever and ever.

I. God's position of authority over Adam

 Theme: God is greater than all and more important than all; He is the highest authority.

Psalm 24:1

Jeremiah 10:23

God is sovereign; He had the right to tell Adam what to do.

— God **made** Adam and gave him his life.

— Adam **belonged** to God.

 Theme: God is love.

Psalm 32:8-10

God told Adam what to do because God is **loving**.

— God wanted to enjoy Adam's love and friendship.

— God only wanted what was best for Adam.

 Theme: God knows everything.

God had the right to tell Adam what to do because God **knows everything**.

Psalm 19:7-11

— God knew what was best for Adam.

— God knew that, if Adam ate the fruit of the tree of the knowledge of good and evil, he would be separated from God, his Creator.

J. Conclusion

 READ Proverbs 1:7.

This is not the same kind of fear with which we fear evil.

No, we fear God because we know that He has told us the truth about sin and the punishment for sin, and He will carry out the punishment just as He has promised.

Just think of who God is!

— God is greater than all.

— He is our Creator.

— He is our owner.

— He knows everything.

— He is holy and righteous; He demands death as the payment for sin.

But God loves us and wants us to be His friends.

He has given us the Bible so we can know Him.

QUESTIONS:

1. Does God ever begin a thing and then not finish it? *No.*

2. Why doesn't God begin things and then leave them unfinished? *Because God never changes. Nothing can stop Him from doing what He plans to do.*

3. Why did God rest on the seventh day? *Because all His work of creating things was finished.*

4. Did God send rain to water the plants when the earth was first created? *No, God watered the plants by mist which rose up from the earth.*

5. For whom did God plant the garden of Eden? *For Adam.*

6. Why was it right for God to put Adam in the garden even though God didn't ask him if he wanted to live there? *God created Adam, so he rightfully belonged to God.*

7. To whom do all things, spirits, and people belong? *To God, their Creator.*

8. Of how many trees in the garden was Adam allowed to eat the fruit? *All of them except one.*

9. Who put the tree of life in the garden for Adam? *God.*

10. What was the name of the tree, the fruit of which God did not want Adam to eat? *The tree of the knowledge of good and evil.*

11. What did God say would happen to Adam if he ate of the fruit from the tree of the knowledge of good and evil? *Adam would die.*

12. What did God mean when He said that man would die?

    a. *Man would be immediately separated from God, the source of his life.*

    b. *His body would die when his soul and spirit were separated from his body.*

    c. *Man's body, soul, and spirit would be separated from God forever in the place which God prepared for Satan and his demons.*

LESSON 7 — Suggestions for Activities

Be sure to allow time to teach the lesson first!

Listed below are carefully designed activities which will help reinforce and focus on the themes you have taught in the lesson. Choose from this list whatever best suits your students and prepare ahead accordingly. The children may participate in these activities during the time remaining after the lesson has been taught.

1. **Memory Verse — Psalm 24:1,2**

   Provide supplies for writing out the verse. Underneath the verse, have the children draw a picture of the earth and many of the things in it.

2. **It Was VERY Good**

   Provide highlighter markers and copies of Genesis 1 for the children. (You could copy the chapter on a copying machine, or encourage them to use their Bibles.)

   Have the children read through Genesis 1 and highlight the words, "It was good" and "It was very good."

   Discuss:

   What did you find that was "good"? What was "very good"?

   What does this word "good" mean? (Stress that everything God made was perfect.)

   Everything God made was perfect. What does this show us about God?

   Reinforce that God is perfect and that everything He does is perfect.

3. **"Seven Days of Creation"**

   Review creation, using the book or classroom poster that the children have worked on in previous lessons.

   Have the children add the words "It was good" and "It was VERY good" to the appropriate pages in their book or on the classroom poster.

   Reinforce that God finished everything He planned to do. This shows that God is faithful.

4. **Who Does This Belong To?**

   Have everyone in the class, including you the teacher and any helpers, place something that belongs to them into a pile. (Ideas: A Bible, a hat, a pencil, a shoe, etc.) Pick up the items one by one. For each, ask: "Who does this belong to? Why?"

   As you are doing this activity, discuss ownership. Ask questions such as:

   Did you make this? Who made it?

Did you buy this? Have you owned it for a long time?

Do I have the right to decide what to do with... (the item you are holding)? Why? Why not?

Return each item to its owner after you discuss it.

Once all the items have been returned, hold up a sheet of paper with the name "Adam" written on it.

Discuss:

Who made Adam? Did God have the right to decide to put Adam in the Garden of Eden? Why?

Reinforce that God created Adam and had the right to put Adam where He wanted him. God is the highest authority.

If you have younger children, you may want to end this activity by gathering the kids into a "pile." One by one, draw a child out of the pile and ask, "Who owns... (Susie)?"

Reinforce that God is the highest authority in our lives because He made us.

5. **Two Choices**

   Provide art supplies for making posters. Have the children draw the Tree of Life and the Tree of Knowledge of Good and Evil in the midst of the Garden of Eden. Have them label the trees on their poster and indicate below each if eating from that tree would be a good choice or a bad choice.

   As they draw or after they finish, discuss:

   God gave Adam clear instructions about what he could and could not eat in the Garden of Eden. What were those instructions? (Genesis 2:16,17)

   Do you remember that God made man in His own image? In what ways was man created in God's image? (Mind, Emotions, Will)

   Why did God make man with a will, that is, the ability to make choices? (So he would choose to love and obey God)

   When God told Adam that he must not eat of the Tree of Knowledge of Good and Evil, what choice did Adam have? (To not eat the fruit or to eat the fruit/To obey or not obey)

   What did God say would happen if Adam disobeyed? (He would die.)

   Reinforce that God made man in His own image with the ability to make choices, yet He clearly communicates with man and tells him what is right and what is wrong. He communicates with us through the Bible. He has given us the Bible so we can know what pleases and displeases Him.

Name _____

GOD CREATED MAN IN HIS IMAGE

GOD CREATED MAN IN HIS IMAGE

Use the words in this WORD BANK to fill in the answer to the questions below. Cross out each word you use so you can see what words have not been used. The finished sentences will tell you a great deal about God and how much He loves man!

love   Adam   in His image   belongs   man   know   obey   earth

Review

1. God prepared the earth for _____.

2. The great difference between the creation of the animals and the creation of man is that God created man _____ _____ _____.

3. God gave man a mind so man could _____ God; God gave man emotions so man could _____ God; God gave man a will so he could _____ God.

4. Who is our very first forefather? _____

5. After God created Adam, the first man, God gave Adam control over the _____ and everything in it.

6. God could give the earth to man because God made the earth and everything _____ to Him.

On the lines below, write out Genesis 1:27 and memorize it. Then see if you can write this verse from memory on the back of this sheet.

_____

_____

_____

_____

_____

Lesson Scripture: Genesis 1:26-31; 2:7   **LESSON 7**   FIRM FOUNDATIONS   **REVIEW SHEET**   © New Tribes Mission, 1993
Permission given to photocopy for classroom use

skit 7 God Placed Adam in Eden

Readers: Uncle Don, Travis, Jessica

Travis:
Guess what! Dad is going to build me a case for my models!

Uncle Don:
That's great! I heard he was going to have an extra week before his next business trip.

Travis:
Guess what else! He's going to teach me some woodworking stuff. He said I might even get to put the finish on the case!

Jessica:
Oh Travis, you're too messy to do that.

Travis:
No, I'm not!

Uncle Don:
Kids! Your dad will probably show you a good way to do it so it won't be quite such a messy job. He really knows how to work with wood.

Travis:
And he's going to teach me to use the handsaw and the electric drill and the sander and some other tools, too. But he won't let me use the power saw.

Jessica:
You'd probably cut yourself.

Travis:
No, I wouldn't!

Jessica:
Yes, you would!

Uncle Don:
Jessica, Travis — that's enough!

Travis:
You should see all the tools he's got. I never knew he had so many. And he knows how to use every one of them. And he's going to teach me!

Jessica:
Well, you're not the only one who gets to do something special. Mom said she and I could bake cookies together for you and Dad!

Uncle Don:
That's great. Your dad and mom really love you and Travis. I know they're glad to have some time to spend with you.

Jessica:
I just wish Dad were home more.

Uncle Don:
So does he. But his job requires him to travel almost all the time.

Travis:
Maybe he'll change his mind about the saw. I'd really like to use that saw. Just think of all the things I could make!

Uncle Don:
Travis, you are going to get yourself into trouble. Your dad made it very clear he doesn't want you using that saw.

Travis:
I know. But it looks like so much fun!

Uncle Don:
Travis, don't you understand? Your dad made that rule **because he loves you**. He knows that you aren't old enough yet to control that saw. It's a very, very dangerous piece of equipment.

Travis:
I think I could handle it!

Uncle Don:
And your dad knows you **couldn't** handle it! Look at all the things he's going to help you learn to do. Why don't you just enjoy those and quit fussing about the saw?

Jessica:
He likes to fuss.

Travis:
So do you.

Jessica:
I do not! Mom won't let me change the oven racks, and I listen to her. I don't want to get burned.

Uncle Don:
Jessica, you're right about obeying your mom, but you do fuss sometimes, don't you!

Jessica:
Well, sometimes.

Uncle Don:
Your parents love you and provide for you and teach you, and they make rules for you because they know what is best for you. I think this would be a good time to look at our Bible story in Genesis. You will see in the Bible that God had that kind of concern for Adam.

Travis:
Do you mean that Adam had to obey God?

Uncle Don:
God did not **make** Adam obey — but He told Adam what was **good** to do and what he **must not do** and **what would happen** if he disobeyed — just like your dad does with you. 📖

lesson

8

God Made Eve

OVERVIEW

This lesson shows God's sovereign creation of woman as a gift to man.

Some points:
— God knew Adam's need for a wife.
— Adam named all the animals but found no suitable companion among them.
— God created the woman from Adam's rib.
— God created the woman perfect because God is perfect.
— God ordained marriage.

LESSON PREPARATION
This section is for you, the teacher.

The passages in the Scripture Reference column are for your own study in preparing for this lesson. Since they may contain concepts that run ahead of the lesson, they are not to be taught at this point.

Note: If you have not taught previously from this series of lessons, please read carefully the note to teachers in the front of this book.

SCRIPTURE: Genesis 2:18-25
LESSON GOALS:

- To show that God in His sovereignty, love, holiness, wisdom, and power provided a wife for Adam.

THIS LESSON SHOULD HELP THE STUDENTS:

- To see God's wisdom and love in providing exactly what we need.
- To see that God values both man and woman very highly.
- To see that marriage was ordained by God.

MEMORY
VERSE
Genesis 23,24

PERSPECTIVE:

In our culture, the sanctity of marriage has been almost obscured by the popular desire to control one's own life and to submit to no one. Sanctity is an appropriate word to describe marriage; "sanctity" means "holiness of life and character...inviolability, sacredness..." (Webster's Dictionary).

A thoughtful look at Scripture is the best way to renew our correct perspective on marriage. This lesson presents God's plan for marriage. If we see that marriage is a union ordained (officially decreed) by God, we cannot consider it outdated (God has not changed His decree regarding marriage), nor can we consider it something just to be tried out to see if it works.

God designed man and woman in His image and gave them sacred responsibilities toward Him and toward each other. If we see ourselves in the light of God's original design for mankind, we will also see ourselves accountable to Him and loved by Him. The self-esteem so earnestly sought by many in our society can only be found in seeing ourselves as related to our Creator.

Many children are suffering the consequences of broken marriages. They need to see that this was not God's plan for man and woman and for marriage and family life. They need to see that God's way is good and perfect. We cannot change their family situations; but we can show them the truth from God's Word and trust God to work in their hearts and to give them hope in Him.

VISUALS:

- Poster 1, "Learning About God" — Use this to emphasize themes.
- Chronological Picture No. 4, Adam and Eve in the Garden

NOTE:

This lesson is short. If you have time remaining at the end of this lesson, you may want to begin Lesson 9, which is a review of all that has been taught thus far.

SPECIAL PREPARATION:

- Make copies for your class of the **Lesson 8 Review Sheet and Skit 8** (at the end of this lesson). Provide pencils for the children.
- Prepare for any activity you select from the **Suggestions for Activities** (at the end of this lesson). As you select activities, remember to allow sufficient time to teach the outlined lesson material.

ON TEACHING THIS LESSON:

You are carefully laying a scriptural foundation on which the Gospel will later be presented. Each lesson builds on previous lessons, so be sure to cover each point carefully.

DON'T COMPLICATE THE MESSAGE!

As you teach, keep in mind that this is a directed study — not an exhaustive survey of the Bible. Keep your lesson on track and moving ahead by limiting and directing any discussion.

Carefully follow the outline. Emphasize the doctrinal themes.

LESSON FORMAT: The **center column** below contains the lesson material to be taught to the students. The **bold outline headings** are only for reference and need not be spoken, as they are incorporated into the outlined material that follows. The material in the **side columns** is for the teacher's own reference and is not intended to be included in the lesson.

TO BE TAUGHT TO THE STUDENTS
(Center Column Only)

LESSON OUTLINE:

REVIEW Lesson 7, using the Lesson 8 Review Sheet.

PERFORM Skit 8. Note: "Uncle Don's" part should be read by an adult.

A. Introduction

How many of you have ever attended a wedding?

Did you know that God was the One who decided that man and woman should marry?

In Genesis 2 we find part of the wedding service spoken in many ceremonies even today.

Men and women and marriage and children are **very** important to God.

But some people don't know or don't believe what God says about marriage.

They say that marriage is something to be tried out to see if it will work — depending on how you feel about it.

— Many people are even suggesting that the idea of marriage is outdated.

But what does the Bible say about marriage?

Let's take a look and find out! Open your Bibles to Genesis 2.

B. God decided that Adam needed a wife to help him and to be his companion.

 Theme: God is greater than all and more important than all; He is the highest authority.

 READ Genesis 2:18.

God decided that Adam should not live alone.

— God was his Creator and knew what was best for him.

— God didn't ask Adam what he wanted or thought best.

— God made the decision to make a wife for Adam.

 Theme: God is love.

God loved Adam and wanted him to be complete.

— God knew that Adam wouldn't continue to be happy if he remained alone.

— Because God loved Adam and wanted the best for him, He decided to make a wife for him.

God knows ahead of time just what our needs will be, and He also knows the best way to meet those needs.

— You will see that He didn't create Adam's wife at the same moment or in the same way He created Adam.

— He created her at just the right time and in just the right way to meet Adam's needs.

Matthew 6:8b

Philippians 4:19

C. God brought all of the animals before Adam to be named by him.

 READ Genesis 2:19,20.

God had placed Adam as master over all the animals, so God also gave Adam the responsibility of giving them all their names. [1]

God brought to Adam every creature He had made, and Adam named them all.

— Consider:

Wouldn't you love to have been there! Imagine all the beautiful animals Adam saw! Imagine having the opportunity to name them all!

D. There was no suitable companion for Adam among the animals.

 Theme: Man needs God.

 READ Genesis 2:20. [2]

[1] Dr. John Whitcomb, a spokesman for biblical creation, has said that Adam's ability to name all the animals gives insight into his perfect intelligence. At this point, Adam had not sinned, so his mind was still in the perfect state in which God had created it. ❏

[2] Note: the KJV words "help meet" means "suitable helper." ❏

God created man very different from the animals.

— Man was made in God's image so he could know, love, and obey God.

— The animals could not know, love, and obey God like man could.

Adam needed someone to whom he could talk and who could do the same things that he could do.

— No animal could be a suitable companion for man.

— He needed someone more like himself.

Man couldn't do anything to provide himself with a companion and wife.

Only God could make a wife for Adam.

God knew that Adam would need a wife; God loved man and did not want him to be alone.

Acts 17:24, 25

E. God created Eve from Adam's rib.

 Theme: God is all-powerful.

 READ Genesis 2:21,22.

Only God could do this.

— He knows everything.

— He can do anything He wants to do.

God made the first woman as a gift for man.

Jeremiah 32:27

— Compare:

If mom or dad gave you a very special gift, should you try to take good care of it? Of course! They gave it to you because they love you, and that gift is especially valuable because of the love with which it was given.

God gave a wife to Adam, and God expected Adam to take good care of her and to love her.

— Consider:

Even though all of the animals must have seemed very interesting (and Adam had seen them all as he named them), imagine how happy Adam must have been to see this lovely woman whom God had made for him! She, like Adam, was created by God, but God had not made her from the dust of the ground as he had made Adam. God had actually made her from part of Adam's own body, Adam's rib. How precious and close she must have been to Adam! And God had given her a mind and emotions and a will, so she also was able to communicate with God and with Adam.

F. Marriage was ordained by God.

 Theme: God is holy and righteous.

 READ Genesis 2:23,24.

[Go over the memory verse several times.]

God made woman for man so they could be married, live together, and have children. **3**

"...Be fruitful, and multiply, and replenish the earth..." (Genesis 1:28).

— This was God's command to Adam.

Consider:

Because God created everything perfect, we can only imagine just how special this woman really was! And God had made her to be that perfect "suitable helper" that Adam needed.

God commanded Adam and Eve to fill the earth and to rule over it. To Adam, uniting with his wife in marriage must have seemed very good indeed!

Marriage was God's perfect plan for Adam and Eve.

— Eve was Adam's gift from God, perfectly suited to Adam's needs.

— Everything that God does and says is good because He is perfect.

He cannot think, say, or do anything evil.

In James 1:17, the Bible tells us that *"Every good gift and every perfect gift is from above, and cometh down from the Father...."*

Marriage is good because God gave marriage to man.

Children and families are very special to God; it was God's idea for a husband and wife to have children.

G. Adam and Eve were unaware that they were naked, and they were totally unembarrassed.

 READ Genesis 2:25.

Adam and Eve were not embarrassed because they had no evil thoughts.

Everything they knew was good, and they had nothing to be ashamed of.

Suggested Visual:

CHRONOLOGICAL PICTURE NO. 4, "ADAM AND EVE IN THE GARDEN"

H. Conclusion

Life was perfect for Adam and Eve.

— God had given them everything they needed.

— Everything around them was beautiful.

— They were able to communicate with God and with each other.

— He had made them rulers over His creation.

3 Children may ask about divorce. Be very sensitive to their questions; they need to know that you care and that God cares. Some may even ask about "live-in" relationships, that is, people who live together but are never formally married. You do not want to get into this kind of discussion, but it would be good to tell them that marriage is God's plan. People have not listened to God, and it makes God very sad. Tell them that God cares and you do too. Offer to talk with them any time after class if they have special questions. ❏

— He was right there with them to guide them in every decision.

— Their work wasn't hard.

— They were perfectly healthy.

What happened?

— We will study later about the terrible things that changed all this peace and beauty.

But God's Word hasn't changed.

— Thousands of years have passed since Adam and Eve became man and wife, but God has never changed what He first wrote about marriage.

QUESTIONS:

1. Who decided that Adam needed a wife? *God did.*

2. Why did God decide to make a wife for Adam? *Because God loved Adam and did not think it was good for Adam to be alone.*

3. Was it right for God to decide to do this without asking Adam? *Yes, God created Adam.*

4. How did God make the first woman? *God put Adam to sleep. He took out one of Adam's ribs. God then made the first woman from Adam's rib.*

5. How was it possible for God to make Eve from one of Adam's ribs? *Nothing is impossible to God. He can do anything He wants to do.*

6. Who told Adam and Eve to marry and to have children? *God, their Creator.*

LESSON 8 — Suggestions for Activities

Be sure to allow time to teach the lesson first!

Listed below are carefully designed activities which will help reinforce and focus on the themes you have taught in the lesson. Choose from this list whatever best suits your students and prepare ahead accordingly. The children may participate in these activities during the time remaining after the lesson has been taught.

1. Memory Verse — Genesis 2:23,24

Cut a large sheet of poster paper into the shape of a heart. With a colored felt-tipped marker, write the memory verses on the heart. Cut the heart into puzzle-shaped pieces. Have the children reassemble the pieces.

If you wish, provide another sheet of poster paper and a glue stick and have the children glue the puzzle to the second sheet. It can then be mounted on the wall to help the children learn the verse.

2. Name That Animal

Bring pictures of animals to class. Try to bring some pictures of animals which are not well-known to the children.

Divide the children into two teams. Flash a picture of an animal before the children. The team which gets the correct answer fastest gets a point. Only one child from each team should respond per picture; the children should take turns so that everyone gets a chance to play. The winning team is the team with the most points.

Remind the children that God gave Adam the responsibility to name all the animals.

3. Different from Man

Discuss the ways animals are different from man.

Man was made in God's image. Do you remember what that means? What about animals? Were they made in God's image? Can they know, love, and obey God like man can?

Man is interested in many things. Do animals have the same interests as man? What are some things that man is interested in that animals are not interested in?

Man has the ability to do many things. What are some abilities that man has that animals do not have? (Communication, creativity, etc.)

Discuss:

Could any animal be a suitable companion for man?

Why not? (Man needed someone like himself, someone to whom he could talk and who could do the same things that he could do.)

Reinforce that God knew that man needed a more appropriate companion than animals and He lovingly provided a wife for him.

4. God Provided ALL That Adam Needed

Provide art supplies to make posters showing how God provided for man. Have the the children divide their posters into two major sections: Physical Needs and Emotional Needs. Under each section, list or draw what God provided.

Discuss:

We have already seen many wonderful things that God created for man. Can you name some of them? (Dry land to walk on, oxygen to breathe, food to eat, trees for shelter, etc.) These marvelous things provided for man's physical needs.

In today's lesson, we saw how God provided for another of man's needs, his emotional needs. Who was the special person that God made for Adam? Why did God make her?

Reinforce that God loved man and did not want him to be alone. God knew that man needed someone to whom he could talk and who could do the same things that he could do.

5. Wedding Announcement

Make "wedding announcements" for Adam and Eve. Write out the words, leaving the underlined part blank for the children to fill in themselves. You could do two announcements on one sheet of 8 1/2" x 11" paper. Make copies for your class, and then cut the sheets in half. Write on the board the words to insert. Let the children fill in the blanks and decorate the announcements.

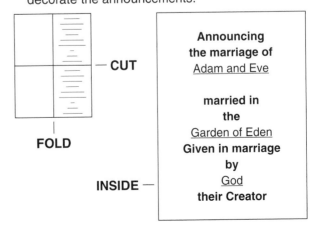

111

Name _____

GOD Placed Adam in Eden

Unscramble the letters to find the words to fill in the blanks.

God always does all He plans to do. God always does what He says. God never _____.
HAGNECS

God rested on the seventh day because all His work of creating was _____.
FDSIHENI

In the beginning, all the plants were watered by a mist or streams from the ground; there was no _____.
NARI

God placed Adam in Eden. He did not ask Adam; He just put Adam in the garden. God could do this because God _____ Adam. Adam rightfully _____ to God.
TEARCDE   **GDELEBON**

Because God created everything and every person, _____ in the world really belongs to God.
YNGERVEHTI

God placed two special trees in the middle of the garden: the tree of life and the tree of knowledge of good and evil.

God told Adam he could eat from all of the trees in the garden except one. In the sentence at the left, find the name of that tree and circle it.

God said that if Adam disobeyed God and ate from the fruit of the tree of knowledge of good and evil, Adam would surely _____. The penalty for sin is death:
EDI

1. Immediately, Adam would be separated from God.

2. Eventually, Adam's body would die.

3. Finally, Adam would be cast into the Lake of Fire, separated from God forever.

Write out Psalm 24:1, 2 and memorize it.

_____

_____

_____

_____

Lesson Scripture: Genesis 2:1-9, 16,17   **LESSON 8**   **REVIEW SHEET**

Travis:
This cold is miserable.

Jessica:
I think I'm catching it too.

Uncle Don:
I've had one myself for about a week now. Kids, did you know that in the beginning there was no sickness?

Travis:
That would be great! You could keep on playing outside no matter what the weather was like!

Uncle Don:
In the beginning, the weather was perfect, too. As a matter of fact, **everything** was perfect. And it was perfect because **God is perfect**, and He created everything perfect and good.

Jessica:
Was Adam perfect too?

Uncle Don:
Yes, Jessica, he was, because God created him perfect. Adam didn't even have to work hard to keep the garden — there weren't any weeds growing.

Travis:
Adam must have been happy!

Uncle Don:
Yes, I think he was. God knew exactly what Adam needed. And He knew that Adam needed a companion, so God made Eve.

Jessica:
Did he make her out of the dust too?

Uncle Don:
No, the Bible tells us here in Genesis that God put Adam to sleep and removed one of Adam's ribs. From that rib, God made the first woman.

Travis:
How did God do that?

Uncle Don:
God knows how to to everything. He is all powerful and he knows everything! Now Adam would not have to be alone. Eve was God's gift to Adam.

Jessica:
You mean God made her just for Adam?

Uncle Don:
That's right — God made Eve to be the perfect helper for Adam.

Jessica:
Were they married?

Uncle Don:
Yes, Jessica, they were. That was God's perfect plan for Adam and Eve. He told them to become just like one person.

Travis:
You mean they were not supposed to be separate any more?

Uncle Don:
That's right, Travis.

Travis:
Did they argue with each other?

Uncle Don:
Not in the beginning. They had perfect friendship with each other and with God. As a matter of fact, God came and talked with them in the garden.

Jessica:
I wonder what the garden was like?

Uncle Don:
It must have been wonderful! Imagine all of the flowers and vegetables and trees and fruits and berries — all the colors and fragrances and sounds and good things to eat — what a place!

Travis:
Did Adam and Eve have to do anything?

Uncle Don:
God gave them the most important job on earth — to be the rulers over everything He had made.

Jessica:
He gave all that to them to take care of?

Uncle Don:
Yes, He did. God made everything for man and He wanted to help them take care of it all.

Travis:
I'd sure like to have seen that garden!

Jessica:
Me too!

Uncle Don:
Yes, it must have been more beautiful than we could ever imagine — well, it was **perfect**, because God is perfect!

Travis:
Uncle Don, the Bible sure tells it better than my science book!

Uncle Don:
The Bible tells the **true story of creation** — God's story. God wants us to know the truth! 📖

lesson

9

FIRM
FOUNDATIONS

Review of Lessons 1-8

This lesson is a review of what has been taught thus far regarding the Bible, God, Satan, and man.

This review is important preparation for Genesis 3, the story of the fall of man, which is covered in following lessons.

LESSON PREPARATION

This section is for you, the teacher.

Note: If you have not taught previously from this series of lessons, please read carefully the note to teachers in the front of this book.

SCRIPTURE: Genesis 1, 2

GENERAL TOPIC:

- Review of what has been taught so far about the Bible, God, Satan, and man.

REVIEWING WHAT HAS BEEN TAUGHT — Some Special Considerations:

As we have taught through Genesis 1 and 2, we have introduced God, Satan, and man, the three main characters in the whole historical drama recorded in the Scriptures. We are now ready to teach Genesis 3, one of the most important chapters in the whole Bible. The origins of man's sinfulness, death, and all earth's miseries, along with the first promise of a Saviour are revealed in Genesis 3. However, the historical and the doctrinal foundational truths of Genesis 3 cannot be grasped apart from a basic understanding of the character of God, Satan, and man. In order to ensure that your students really do comprehend, Lesson 9 is a review of the main points already taught about these three persons. Also included are some questions emphasizing the authority of God's Word, the Bible.

Review by asking questions.

1. If you ask a question and they cannot answer or give a wrong answer, ask some other relevant question or give them some clues. If they cannot answer after a little help, go ahead and tell them. Do not rebuke them if they do not know the answer, and be careful not to embarrass anyone by belaboring the question.

2. If you have several students, direct some questions to the whole group and others to individuals.

3. If one or two people are answering most of the questions, you may want to go around the group, one by one, giving each person the opportunity to answer. Be careful not to embarrass anyone by pressing for answers.

4. If your class is very small and you have older students, you may want to give each student a question sheet and talk through the questions less formally. You still need their feedback, and this will keep you from having to do all the asking if they can look at the sheet with you.

5. Some of these questions involve controversial issues. You may have older students who want to debate these issues. Let them know that you appreciate their interest, but let them know, too, that the purpose of the class is not debate. Many of these issues have been debated in the past and undoubtedly will be in the future. But the purpose of the class is to show what the Bible says and to learn the Word of God accurately. Whatever you

do, be sure to limit discussion of these controversial subjects. Winning an argument will not help convince a heart. Just allow the Holy Spirit to use the truth and be firm but loving and patient with those who disagree.

Review is extremely important; don't skip it just to save time. Reviewing will help to solidify information in the students' minds and will help you as a teacher to know how well you are communicating and what areas need extra attention as you continue to teach. No matter how well you may have said it, the proof of the teaching will lie in what your students have learned! And an excellent way to know what's been learned is to ask questions.

REVIEW GAMES

Depending upon your class, you may want to have some competition in answering these questions. Most children love to compete, and it keeps their attention. One way is to divide the class into teams and just have points. The team with the most questions answered correctly wins. This works well with more than two teams. Or, if you only have two teams, you may want to use a tic-tac-toe game instead of points, and allow the child who answers correctly to write in the "X" or the "O" for his team.

If you decide to make teams and compete, alternate teams with your questions. If one team can't answer a question, let the next team have the opportunity to answer that question. The question needs to be answered by the person who raises his hand first. Then, if he is wrong, the other team gets the opportunity to try to answer. Everyone but the person who raises his hand first must be quiet. The order of new questions remains the same, regardless of which team answered the question. For example, if team A was originally asked the question but had the wrong answer, and B is given the question, the next question will still go to team B, and so on.

NOTE: The discussion questions are not appropriate for games. If you are doing review games, you may want to go through all the other questions first and then after the games cover the discussion questions.

ON TEACHING THIS LESSON:

You are carefully laying a scriptural foundation on which the Gospel will later be presented. Each lesson builds on previous lessons, so be sure to cover each point carefully.

DON'T COMPLICATE THE MESSAGE!

As you teach, keep in mind that this is a directed study — not an exhaustive survey of the Bible. Keep your lesson on track and moving ahead by limiting and directing any discussion.

Carefully follow the outline. Emphasize the doctrinal themes.

The center column on the following pages contains the questions to be asked of the students. The material in the side columns is for the teacher's own reference and is not intended to be included in the lesson.

TO BE TAUGHT TO THE STUDENTS
(Center Column Only)

LESSON OUTLINE:

REVIEW Lesson 8, using the Lesson 9 Review Sheet.

PERFORM Skit 9. Note: "Uncle Don's" part should be read by an adult.

A. The Bible

Before we learn any more about the story of Adam and Eve, we are going to review what we have already learned about the Bible, God, Satan, and the first man and woman God created. We will begin by asking you some questions about God's Word, the Bible.

1. Who is the author of the Bible? *God.*

2. Whom did God use to write down the Bible? *He used over 40 men, all of whom were Jewish except one.*

3. To whom is the Bible written? *To everyone in the whole world.*

4. Has the Bible changed over the years since it was first written? *No. The Bible has not changed and never will.*

5. God's Word was written down over a period of how many years? *1,600 years.*

OPTIONAL DISCUSSION QUESTION:

6. Why has God given us the Bible? *He wants to communicate with us — He wants us to know Him, and He wants us to know how to live.*

B. God

1. In your own words, define what we mean when we say God is sovereign. *God is greater than all and more important than all; He is the highest authority.*

2. Does God have a material body? *No, He is Spirit, and does not have flesh and bones as we do.*

3. Was there ever a time when God wasn't living? *No.*

4. Does God change or could God die? *No, God is always the same. He can never die, for He is eternal.*

5. We need food, water, air, the earth to walk on, and the sun to warm us, but what does God need? *God doesn't need anything.*

6. How then does God live? *He lives by His own power.*

7. Where is God? *God is everywhere all the time.*

8. How many Gods are there? *There is only one God.*

9. Who are the three persons who are this one God? *God the Father, God the Son, and God the Holy Spirit.*

10. What did God use to make the heavens and the earth? *God didn't use anything. He made everything out of nothing.*

11. How did God create everything? *By speaking and commanding them to appear.*

12. How could God make the heavens and the earth? *God is almighty. There is nothing He cannot do. He knows everything and has the power to do anything.*

13. What did God say about everything that He made? *He said that everything was very good.*

14. Why could God make everything perfect? *Because He is perfect.*

15. Why did God prepare such variety and beauty and make so many good things on the earth for man? *Because God is loving and kind.*

16. When scientists and engineers speak of physical laws, whose laws are these? *God established all the physical laws of the universe. Man is only using what God made.*

17. Why is God the rightful owner of everything? *He created all things, and He gave everything life.*

18. Why does God have the right to demand obedience from us? *Because He is our Creator and owner.*

THE FOLLOWING ARE OPTIONAL DISCUSSION QUESTIONS. [1]

20. Considering what you have already learned about God, what do you think of statements like these:

    a. "The Man Upstairs"

    b. "Everyone has to find a `higher power.'"

    c. "Religion is a personal thing; everyone is entitled to his own opinion about God."

21. Many people believe that everything came into being by chance. What does the Bible say? *The Bible says God created everything, and that He did it in a very systematic way. Chance was not involved in creation.*

22. Many people believe that man evolved. What does the Bible tell us in Genesis 1 and 2? *The Bible tells us that man was created special and different from all the rest of creation: man was created in God's image. God breathed into man the breath of life; Eve was created from Adam's rib. No "evolutionary process" is mentioned or hinted at.*

23. Give some evidences from things you can see around you and from what you know about the Bible that show that life was created rather than evolved. *Animals, plants, man all have complex systems that could not have happened by chance. Cats have kittens; dogs have puppies — all types of animals have babies after their own kind. The Bible is true history, not a book of theories. The Bible says God created everything. The Bible has not changed through the centuries; man's theories are constantly changing.*

24. God has shown us a great deal about Himself by what He has made — every day we see His creation and should know that One greater than us has done these things. You have also learned many things about God's character through what we have studied so far in His Word. What things in particular stand out to you about God's character?

1 These are helpful if you have students who are a little older. If you use this type of discussion questions, be careful to keep the discussion under control. Students should be given opportunity to express their opinion briefly and not be put down for what they think. But do not let someone dominate the discussion, especially with wrong answers.

You are trying to make your students evaluate their own ideas from the past in light of what they are learning.

Be patient with them.

If someone says of another student's answer, "That's wrong!" you might reply, "Well, we are just asking for opinions now. What do **you** think? ❏

C. Satan

1. Where did all the spirits come from? *They were all created by God.*

2. Did God create the spirits with bodies of flesh and bones? *No.*

3. Did God create all of the spirits good, or did He create some good and some bad? *God created them all good.*

4. Why did God create the spirits? *To be His servants.*

5. Where did they all live in the beginning when God first created them? *With God in Heaven.*

6. Are each of the spirits everywhere at the same time like God is? *No. There are spirits all over the world, but they cannot be in all places at the same time like God.*

7. Who was the most intelligent and beautiful angel created by God? *Lucifer.*

8. What position did God give Lucifer? *Leadership over all of the other angels.*

9. Whom was Lucifer to serve and obey? *God, his Creator.*

10. What did Lucifer plan to do? *He planned to be like God and to take God's position.*

11. Who else followed Lucifer in his rebellion against God? *Many of God's angels.*

12. What did God do? *God removed Lucifer and the angels who joined him in rebellion from their position as God's servants.*

13. What is Lucifer's name now and what does it mean? *Satan, which means enemy, opponent, accuser.*

14. What place of punishment did God prepare for Satan and his demons? *The Lake of Fire as their future place of punishment.*

15. Whom is Satan against? *He is against God and everything which God loves.*

D. Man

1. What great difference was there between the creation of man and the creation of animals? *God made man in His image.*

2. What does it mean that God made man in His image? *God made man like Himself with a mind so man could know God, emotions so man could love God, and a will so man could choose to obey God.*

3. Was man good or bad when God created him? *Man was good.*

4. After the first man Adam was created, over what did God give him control? *The earth and everything in it.*

119

5. Where did God place Adam after He created him? *In a beautiful garden called Eden which God Himself prepared for Adam.*

7. What two very important trees did God also place in the garden of Eden? *The tree of life and the tree of the knowledge of good and evil.*

8. God told Adam that he must not eat of the fruit of which tree? *The tree of the knowledge of good and evil.*

9. What did God say would happen to man if he disobeyed and ate the fruit of the tree of the knowledge of good and evil? *God said that man would die.*

10. What did God mean when He said that man would die?

    a. *Man would be separated immediately from God, the source of his life. His friendship with God would be broken.*

    b. *His body would die when his soul and spirit were separated from his body.*

    c. *Man's body, soul, and spirit would be separated from God forever in the place which God prepared for Satan and his demons.*

11. Whom did God create for Adam after He placed Adam in the garden of Eden? *God created Eve to be Adam's wife.*

12. Why did God create Eve? *God loved Adam, and did not want him to be alone. As no animal would be a suitable companion, God made someone special for Adam. Also, God wanted man to have children.*

13. Describe Eve's God-given role at the time God created her. *She was to be Adam's helper, a companion for him so he would not be lonesome. She was also commanded, with Adam, to rule over all of the other creatures God had made and to be fruitful and fill the earth and subdue it.*

14. Was Adam the only one who could communicate with God? *No, Eve was also created in God's image and given a mind and emotions and a will so she could communicate with God and with Adam.*

OPTIONAL DISCUSSION QUESTION:

15. In light of what we've learned about God and man, what do you think about these statements:

    a. "Do your own thing!"

    b. "I don't answer to anybody!"

    c. "I can do whatever I want with my life, because it belongs to me."

Name _____

GOD Made Eve

Use the words in the word bank on the right to fill in the blanks in the sentences below

WORD BANK

God
all-powerful
loved
authority
God
marry
Adam's
children

1. _____ decided that Adam needed a wife as a companion.

2. God decided to make a wife for Adam because God _____ Adam and did not think it was good for Adam to be alone.

3. It was right for God to make a wife for Adam without asking Adam first, because God is the final _____ over every person and everything.

4. God made the first woman from one of _____ ribs.

5. God was able to make Eve from one of Adam's ribs, because nothing is impossible for God. He is _____-_____.

6. God told Adam and Eve to _____ and have _____.

7. At this time, marriage was good and happy because Adam and Eve were living just the way _____ told them to live.

Can you write out Genesis 1:27 from memory? Look in your Bible if you need help.

_____
_____
_____
_____

Jessica:
Uncle Don, I'm sure glad we moved next door to you!

Travis:
Me, too!

Uncle Don:
I'm really glad too! It's a lot of fun to get to know you kids. If you hadn't moved here, we would hardly know each other right now.

Jessica:
That's right! We didn't live that far away before, but we never got together.

Travis:
Now we see you just about every day.

Uncle Don:
And I love it!

Travis:
I never knew you knew so much about gardening. Would you believe it — that science project you helped me with — I got an A!

Uncle Don:
You did the work. I'm glad you enjoyed it. I've learned a lot about you too — Jessica loves to bake cookies and Travis loves to eat cookies!

Travis:
You're right!

Jessica:
I brought some! Do you want some now?

Uncle Don:
That's great, Jessica! Thank you. We can have some before we have our lesson.

Jessica:
That's another thing I learned about you — I didn't know you liked to read so much. You are always reading your Bible!

Uncle Don:
You know, Jessica, it's just like our visits. We've learned about each other because we are spending time together. Like you said, we used to live fairly close, but we never got together.

Travis:
But now we're seeing each other and learning a lot about each other! May I have a cookie?

Uncle Don:
Sure, Travis. Jessica, these are good. I'll bet you and your mom have a good time baking together.

Jessica:
I love it! Mom is a lot of fun.

Uncle Don:
And you really enjoyed working on that wood project with your dad, didn't you, Travis.

Travis:
That was great! I didn't realize all the things my dad could do! I just kept watching him and watching him. He's really good with tools.

Uncle Don:
You know, you kids have been learning a lot, being with your parents and watching them work. I think you might be surprised how much you are learning about someone else, too.

Jessica:
Who is that?

Uncle Don:
Well, I was thinking about God!

Travis:
God?

Uncle Don:
Yes! We've been reading about the things God did in creating everything. I think we've already learned quite a bit about Him. Let's see — what do you know about where God is?

Travis:
He's everywhere — all the time!

Uncle Don:
Very good! How great is He?

Jessica:
He's the greatest! No one is as great as God!

Uncle Don:
You are right, Jessica. God is greater than all. Was there ever a time when God was not living?

Travis:
No, He's always been alive.

Jessica:
He always will be! He's eternal!

Uncle Don:
What does God need in order to exist?

Jessica:
He doesn't need anything!

Uncle Don:
What did God use to make everything?

Travis:
He didn't use anything! He just spoke! You know what? We **are** learning a lot about God!

Uncle Don:
Yes, you are. God is **wonderful** and there's so much more to learn about Him!

lesson
10   Adam and Eve Disobeyed God

FIRM
FOUNDATIONS

OVERVIEW

**This lesson presents
Satan's deception of Eve
and Adam's disobedience
of God's command.**

Considered in this lesson:

— Satan's characteristics
   and tactics.

— The immediate result
   of Adam and Eve's sin
   — separation from God.

LESSON PREPARATION
This section is for you, the teacher.

The passages in the Scripture Reference column are for your own study
in preparing for this lesson. Since they may contain concepts that run
ahead of the lesson, they are not to be taught at this point.

**Note: If you have not taught previously from this series of lessons,
please read carefully the note to teachers in the front of this book.**

SCRIPTURE: Genesis 3:1-8

LESSON GOALS:

• To show Satan's hatred for God and for man, and Satan's character as a
  liar, deceiver, accuser, and murderer.

• To show man's choice to willfully disobey God and the immediate results of
  that sin.

THIS LESSON SHOULD HELP THE STUDENTS:

• To see that Satan is God's enemy and the student's enemy.

• To recognize some of Satan's schemes.

• To realize the need to know and believe God's Word.

• To see the terrible consequences of sin.

PERSPECTIVE FOR THE TEACHER:

Many people in our society think that they know a great deal about the Bible.
They have heard about God; they have heard about Adam and Eve and the garden;
they have heard about Adam and Eve's sin; they have heard about Satan.

But to many people, these things they have heard are only a story or a myth.
They may have been taught to view the story of Adam and Eve as an allegory. Or
they might even tell you that they believe the Bible, but in actuality, they have not
taken the time to read or study God's Word nor have they allowed what little they
have heard to have any application in their own lives.

We have a tremendous obligation to the Lord and to the children we teach to
present this passage of Scripture clearly as God's truth. This is no simple story of
an "apple" and a snake and a woman. Instead, this is the critical point of all human
history before the coming of Christ.

VISUALS:

• Chronological Picture No. 4, "Adam and Eve in the Garden"

• Chronological Picture No. 5, "The Fall of Man"

• Chronological Picture No. 6, "Fig Leaf Coverings"

• Poster 4, "God and Man" (See instruction sheet with posters)

• Poster 1, "Learning About God" — Use this to emphasize the themes.

• The tree branch that was used with Lesson 7

MEMORY
VERSE
Psalm 119:160

SPECIAL PREPARATION:

- Make copies for your class of the **Lesson 10 Review Sheet** and **Skit 10** (at the end of this lesson). Provide pencils for the children.
- Prepare for any activity you select from the **Suggestions for Activities** (at the end of this lesson). As you select activities, remember to allow sufficient time to teach the outlined lesson material.

ON TEACHING THIS LESSON:

You are carefully laying a scriptural foundation on which the Gospel will later be presented. Each lesson builds on previous lessons, so be sure to cover each point carefully.

DON'T COMPLICATE THE MESSAGE!

As you teach, keep in mind that this is a directed study — not an exhaustive survey of the Bible. Keep your lesson on track and moving ahead by limiting and directing any discussion.

Carefully follow the outline. Emphasize the doctrinal themes.

LESSON FORMAT: The **center column** below contains the lesson material to be taught to the students. The **bold outline headings** are only for reference and need not be spoken, as they are incorporated into the outlined material that follows. The material in the **side columns** is for the teacher's own reference and is not intended to be included in the lesson.

TO BE TAUGHT TO THE STUDENTS
(Center Column Only)

LESSON OUTLINE:

The Lesson 10 Review Sheet is a take-home poster of the attributes of God. The children can color it while you are waiting for all the students to arrive or take it home to color. You will review the situation in the Garden of Eden with verbal questions after the skit and introduction.

PERFORM Skit 10. Note: "Uncle Don's" part should be read by an adult.

A. Introduction

Today we're going to study one of the most important events in all of history.

This one event **affected everyone who has ever lived!**

We're going to start by asking some questions to remind ourselves of what had already taken place:

1. Where did God place Adam after He created him? *In a beautiful garden called Eden which God Himself prepared for Adam.*

2. What two very important trees did God also place in the garden of Eden? *The tree of life and the tree of the knowledge of good and evil.*

3. God told Adam that he must not eat of the fruit of which tree? *The tree of the knowledge of good and evil.*

4. What did God say would happen to man if he disobeyed and ate the fruit of the tree of the knowledge of good and evil? *God said that man would die.*

5. What did God mean when He said that man would die?

   a. *Man would be separated immediately from God, the source of his life. His friendship with God would be broken.*

   b. *His body would die when his soul and spirit were separated from his body.*

   c. *Man's body, soul, and spirit would be separated from God forever in the place which God prepared for Satan and his demons.*

6. Whom did God create for Adam after He placed Adam in the garden of Eden? *God created Eve to be Adam's wife.*

7. Why did God create Eve? *Because there was no animal that was a suitable companion for Adam and because God loved him, He did not want Adam to be alone. God wanted man to have children.*

B. Life in the Garden of Eden

Life in the garden was pleasant for Adam and Eve; everything was perfect.

Suggested Visual:

CHRONOLOGICAL PICTURE NO. 4, "ADAM AND EVE IN THE GARDEN"

— They had everything that they needed.

— God was their friend; He loved them, and they were very happy.

DISPLAY THE POSTER, "GOD AND MAN," USING ONLY SECTIONS 4A AND 4B, SIDE BY SIDE WITH NO SEPARATION.

They had perfect friendship and fellowship with God and with each other.

But what about God's great enemy, Satan?

— Satan knew about God's warning to Adam concerning the tree of the knowledge of good and evil.[1]

— Because Satan hates God, he wanted to destroy the man and woman that God had made.

— Therefore, Satan planned to deceive Eve. (To deceive means to trick or fool.)

[1] We know that Satan was aware of this warning because he falsely restated it to Eve (Genesis 3:1). ❑

C. Satan used the serpent to disguise himself and deceive Eve.

 Theme: Satan fights against God and His will. Satan is a liar and a deceiver. He hates man.

 READ Genesis 3:1.

This wasn't just a snake talking to Eve.

— Satan himself had entered into the snake.

— He disguised himself as a snake so he could deceive (trick) Eve.

Satan is a deceiver.

— He didn't allow Eve to know that he was the one talking through the snake.

— The more you learn from God's Word, the more you realize how deceitful and wicked Satan is.

   He knows that he is lying.

   John 8:44 says that Satan is a liar and a murderer.

   He wants everyone to go to the place of eternal punishment, the Lake of Fire.

   His name means "deceiver" or "accuser."

— The Bible says that Satan can appear as *"an angel of light."*

   This is what Satan did to Eve: he deceived her by coming to her in the form of a snake.

   Up until that time, the animals had not been harmful in any way to Adam and Eve or to each other, so Eve was not afraid.

II Corinthians 11:14

D. Satan still deceives people.

Satan is still trying to deceive and destroy people. [2]

He doesn't use a serpent like he did with Eve, but he uses whatever ways people will accept.

Many times Satan deceives and tricks people by speaking lies right into their minds.

— Explain:
   — *Actually, Satan himself can only be in one place at one time. But, you may remember that many of the angels followed Satan in his rebellion against God. God removed Satan and his rebellious followers from their positions of service to God in Heaven. These rebellious angels, called demons, now roam the earth unseen and work with Satan speaking lies in people's minds against God and against men.*

— Satan doesn't want anyone to know or to believe God.

— He may put a question into your mind such as, "Why should I believe the Bible?"

— Sometimes Satan uses other people through whom he speaks his lies to us.

Satan lies to us and tries to trick us, just as he lied to Eve and tricked her.

Acts 5:3

II Corinthians 4:4

[2] This section is not intended to frighten the children, but to help them identify the Enemy.

Most children will actually appreciate knowing Satan's characteristics — they are daily bombarded by his schemes, and it is helpful for them to know where these evil things originate.

At this point you are not teaching them how to behave; you are giving them foundational teaching on the characteristics of Satan and how he works to deceive people. The children need to know that this ancient Deceiver is still the same today. ❑

— He tries to make us feel that we will miss out on something if we don't follow along.

— He tries to make us think he has something good for us.

— He tells us that he knows something better than God or our parents or our teachers have told us.

When we have believed Satan's lies, we find out too late that what looked so good was really something very evil.

Satan wants to destroy us.

What are some of his lies?

— Anything that tells you to rebel against God, your parents, or your teachers or other authorities that God has placed over you.

— Anything that claims to predict the future, such as horoscopes and ouija boards.

— Anything that makes evil seem good or fun or funny.

— Games or music or anything else that brags about evil or tells you to lie, steal, say bad words, or do anything evil.

— Anything that denies God or the truth of the Bible.

All of these kinds of things are really from Satan.

E. Satan tempted and deceived Eve.

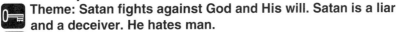 **Theme: Satan fights against God and His will. Satan is a liar and a deceiver. He hates man.**

 READ Genesis 3:1.

Why did Satan ask Eve this question?

— He already knew the correct answer.

— He didn't care what God had said.

— He was testing Eve so he could trick her.

— He was trying to make her **doubt God's Word** — this is one of Satan's favorite tricks.

 Theme: God communicates with man.

 READ Genesis 3:2,3.

Satan had already confused Eve.

Her answer was not what God had said.

— God did not say they could not **touch** the fruit.

— He had said they must not **eat** it.

God's command was for both Adam and Eve.

— God first gave this command to Adam.

— Adam apparently told Eve what God had said.

— Whatever God said to Adam included Eve.

 READ Genesis 3:4,5.

Now Satan was calling God a liar.

Satan himself is really the liar.

— Consider:

God had said: "If you eat the fruit from the tree of the knowledge of good and evil, you will die that same day." God

*meant that Adam and Eve would be cut off from God, the
One who gave them life. God said, "You will die." Satan said,
"You will not die." Satan was lying.*

What was really behind Satan's lie?

— Satan had rebelled against God's authority.

He sinned when he wanted to take God's place.

He didn't want to obey God anymore.

— Now Satan was suggesting to Eve that she should rebel
against God.

Satan was suggesting that she should eat the fruit so
that she could be like God in knowing what was good
and what was evil.

Satan wanted Eve to believe that she wouldn't need God
to tell her what was right and what was wrong.

But here is the truth:

— God didn't make people to live by their own ideas and
thoughts.

— God made us to be guided by His own Word.

F. Eve ate and also gave the fruit to Adam.

 **Theme: Man is a sinner. He needs God and is helpless to
save himself.**

 READ Genesis 3:6.

Suggested Visual:

CHRONOLOGICAL PICTURE NO. 5,
"THE FALL OF MAN"

Satan deceived Eve.

— She believed that Satan was telling the truth.

— She believed that she would be wise like God.

I Timothy
2:14

Even though Adam knew that God had said not to eat, he deliberately disobeyed God's command.

— Adam turned away from depending on God.

He wanted to be independent of God.

He wanted to decide for himself what was good and what
was evil.

Adam didn't want God to rule over him anymore.

Did God have the right to rule over Adam?

— Yes, God was his Creator.

— Everything he had came from God.

Does God have the right to tell us what to do?

— Yes, all that we have comes from God; He gave us life.

I Chroni-
cles
29:11,12

Psalm
24:1

G. Adam and Eve's sin separated them from God.

 Theme: God is faithful; He always does what He says; He never changes.

 READ Genesis 3:7,8.

What did God say would happen to them if they ate of the tree of the knowledge of good and evil?

What did God mean by "die"?

— They didn't drop dead immediately when they ate the fruit.

— They were still walking around.

— They were making themselves coverings out of leaves.

— Does this mean that God's Word didn't come true?

— Was Satan right after all?

No! They were separated from God immediately when they ate the fruit.

— God always does what He says.

— He never changes.

— He doesn't forget His threats to punish disobedience of His commands.

 Theme: God is holy and righteous. He demands death as the payment for sin.

Why did their sin separate them from God?

 READ Isaiah 59:2: *"But **your iniquities** [sins] **have separated between you and your God**, and your sins have hid his face from you, that he will not hear."* [3]

[3] The boldfaced portion of the verse is the part you are to emphasize. Don't get sidetracked. ❏

— Because God is holy and righteous, He will not continue in friendship with those who disobey His commands.

— He hates everything that is wrong and punishes all disobedience of His commands by death.

— Romans 6:23 says, *"...the wages of sin is death...."*

Because Adam and Eve disobeyed God, they were cut off from their friendship with God.

— Their relationship with God was dead.

ON THE POSTER "GOD AND MAN," COVER "man" WITH 4C, AND SEPARATE MAN AND GOD BY PLACING 4D BETWEEN 4A AND 4B

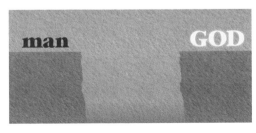

— They were no longer in oneness with God.

— They had taken sides with God's great enemy, Satan, and they, too, were now the enemies of God.

DISPLAY BRANCH BROKEN OFF FROM A TREE.

Look at this branch. It didn't turn completely brown the minute it was broken off from the tree. It still has some green in it. But it is dying because it is cut off from its source of life.

The same thing happened to Adam and Eve. They didn't drop dead on the day they disobeyed God. They were still breathing and walking around. But they had died to God. That part of them which was made in God's image so they could know, love, and obey Him was immediately separated from God when they disobeyed His command. They were now separated from Him and had become the enemies of God. Their bodies would also eventually die, and they would go to the place of everlasting punishment which God prepared for Satan and the evil spirits.

H. Signs of separation from God

These were the signs that they were now separated from God:

— First, their attitude toward their bodies changed immediately.

Before they disobeyed God, they were naked, but they felt no embarrassment.

Now they were separated from God, and their minds were no longer under God's control.
— Their minds became evil, and their attitude toward their bodies changed.
— They were embarrassed by their naked bodies.

— Secondly, they tried to provide their own needs.

Before they were separated from God, they looked to God to provide everything they needed.

But now they tried to do things for themselves.

— They clothed themselves with fig leaves.

— They no longer trusted God to give them what they needed.

— Perhaps they reasoned that if they clothed themselves, God wouldn't notice that anything had happened.

TO THE POSTER, GOD AND MAN, ADD OUTWARD APPEARANCE.

— But God does not accept us based upon our outward appearance.

— *Consider:*

Just as Adam and Eve tried to make themselves acceptable to God by putting on clothes, many people today think they can make themselves acceptable to God by doing things that make them look good. Here are some examples:

— *Doing good deeds*

— *Joining the church*
— *Giving to charities.*
—I Samuel 16:7 says, *"...man looketh on the outward appearance, but the LORD looketh on the heart."*

— Adam and Eve not only tried to cover their nakedness, but when God came to visit Adam and Eve, they also tried to hide from Him.

Suggested Visual:

CHRONOLOGICAL PICTURE NO. 6, "FIG LEAF COVERINGS"

 Theme: God is loving, merciful, and gracious.

— Compare:

Do you like to visit with your friends? God loved Adam and Eve, and so He came at the close of the day to talk with them.

Before they were separated from God, they loved Him and wanted to talk with Him. But when God came after they had disobeyed Him, Adam and Eve hid.

— Compare:

Have you ever done something wrong and then hidden when your mom or dad came near? Have you ever tried to cover up for something wrong you've done? Yes, all of us have done that, just like Adam and Eve.

Sin — disobedience to God — brings fear and shame and causes people to turn away from God.

— When God created Adam and Eve, they didn't fear anything.

There was nothing in the world to fear.
God was their friend.
No animals would hurt them.
All the world was good and beautiful.
Sickness and death did not exist.

Hebrews 2:15

— Disobedience to God is the reason that we have fear in the world today.

Ever since Adam and Eve disobeyed God, there has been terrible fear in the hearts of men, women, and children.

— Can you think of some things people are afraid of?
Sickness
Death
Money problems
Robbers
War

 Theme: God is faithful; He always does what He says; He never changes.

— Do you think that Adam and Eve should have been afraid of God?

Would God really punish them for their disobedience?

Or is God like many people who only make idle threats?

— Compare:

Have your parents ever threatened to punish you for something and then not done it? Maybe they forgot, or maybe they were just too busy.

But do you think God is like that? Did God merely threaten Lucifer and the angels when they rebelled? No! God always does exactly as He has promised to do.

Had Adam and Eve been warned of the consequences of sin?

— Yes! God had clearly warned them.

— The devil did not "make them do it"; they **chose** to sin.

Now Adam and Eve had good reason to be afraid of God.

Why? Because they had disobeyed God, their Creator.

— They depended upon God for everything.

— The very breath that they had in their bodies was given by God.

— But Adam had deliberately disobeyed God's command.

— God always punishes those who disobey any of His commands.

Theme: God is everywhere all the time; He knows everything.

Were Adam and Eve able to hide from God?

No! God saw Adam and Eve when they were trying to hide.

Can anyone hide from God?

Is there anywhere we can go where God is not already there?

No! God is everywhere.

— No one can hide from Him.

— God has heard and seen everything that we have said and done from the day that we were born.

I. Conclusion

What you have just heard is the true story of how man became separated from God.

— Adam and Eve were separated from God because of their sin.

— They were separated from Him immediately, just as He said they would be.

God always tells the truth.

He always does exactly what He says.

But Satan is a liar and a murderer.

— He is not the cartoon character with the pitchfork and red suit who is easy to identify.

— He is the Deceiver, the enemy of our souls.

Genesis 2:7

Acts 17:25

Psalm 139

Jeremiah 23:23, 24

QUESTIONS:

1. When Satan came to deceive Eve, did he come and talk to her face-to-face so she could see him and know who he was? *No.*

2. What did Satan use to disguise himself when he spoke to Eve? *A snake.*

3. God told Adam that, if they ate the fruit from the tree of the knowledge of good and evil, they would definitely die, but Satan told Eve they would not. What was Satan suggesting God to be? *A liar.*

4. What did Satan tell Eve would happen to them? *Satan said that they would not die but that they would become like God and be able to decide for themselves what is good and what is evil.*

5. Does Satan still try to deceive and trick people? *Yes.*

6. Does Satan want you to listen to and believe God's words? *No.*

7. God said that Adam and Eve would die if they ate of the fruit of the tree of the knowledge of good and evil. Satan said they would not die. Who spoke the truth? *God did.*

8. Satan is very strong. Was it all his fault that Adam and Eve sinned? *No. Adam and Eve chose to sin. God had made His instructions clear to them; He had been very loving to them. He gave them a will to make choices; they chose to disobey.*

9. Adam and Eve didn't fall dead immediately when they ate the fruit of the tree of the knowledge of good and evil. God had said they would die for their disobedience. What did He mean?

   a. *They would immediately be separated from God, the source of their life — their relationship with God would die right then.*

   b. *Their bodies would eventually die because of their disobedience.*

   c. *They would eventually be separated from God forever — body, soul, and spirit — in the Lake of Fire.*

10. What did Adam and Eve do when they realized they were naked? Why did they do this? *They made clothes of leaves because their attitudes toward their bodies had changed. They tried to take care of their own needs instead of asking God to help them.*

11. What did Adam and Eve do when they heard God coming to see them? Why did they do this? *They hid because they no longer felt comfortable in God's presence. Their attitude toward Him had changed because of their sin, and they were no longer His friends. They were ashamed and afraid.*

12. Is it possible to hide from God? *No, God is everywhere.*

133

LESSON 10 — Suggestions for Activities

Be sure to allow time to teach the lesson first!

Listed below are carefully designed activities which will help reinforce and focus on the themes you have taught in the lesson. Choose from this list whatever best suits your students and prepare ahead accordingly. The children may participate in these activities during the time remaining after the lesson has been taught.

1. **Memory Verse — Psalm 119:160**
   As the children learn this verse, emphasize that God's Word is **true** and **eternal**.

2. **True or False**
   Present statements to the class (samples below) to point out the type of lies Satan uses to try to deceive people. Ask the children if the statement is True or False. (Use statements that your children can relate to. The statements should all be false.) Have the children make up a true statement to counter each lie. (Note: the emphasis here is not on doing "good deeds" or on "right behaviour." Rather, the emphasis is on seeing the lie, having understood the truth from what has been taught so far from God's Word.)

   Sample statements:

   1) "It is much more important to play in today's soccer game than it is to go to Bible class." (Counter the lie with a true statement, such as, "Studying the Bible is the most important thing because through the Bible I can learn about God.")

   2) "The Bible is full of myths. It isn't really true."

   3) "The world evolved over a long period of time."

   4) "You are so smart. You don't need God."

   5) "You don't need to listen to God, or to your parents, or to your teachers, or any other authorities that are over you. Nobody does!"

   6) "It's fine for you to read this horoscope. It's going to tell you exactly what's going to happen to you today."

   7) "Sure, this music video brags about evil, but that's fine. These musicians are the BEST, and everybody listens to them."

   Reinforce that Satan is a liar and a deceiver.

3. **What did God Really Say?**
   This activity will help the children see the discrepancies between what Satan and Eve said about eating the fruit of the tree of knowledge of good and evil compared to what God had said. Before class, prepare a poster (or handouts) with three columns, titled "What God Said," "What Satan Said," and "What Eve Said." Write what each said in the correct section (either before class or as you come to it in the following discussion).

   Discuss:

   Let's read in our Bibles what these different ones said about eating from the tree of the knowledge of good and evil.

   First, what had God told Adam in Genesis 2:16,17? (Write these words on the poster.)

   What question did Satan ask in Genesis 3:1 to cast doubt on God's Word?

   What did Eve reply in Genesis 3:2,3? (Write these words on the poster.) How was Eve's reply different from what God had said? (Have the children highlight the words that are different.)

   What did Satan say in Genesis 3:4,5? (Write these words on the poster.) How was this different from what God said? (Have the children highlight the words that are different.)

   Who was telling the truth?

   Reinforce that God communicates with man. Reinforce also that Satan is a liar and a deceiver.

4. **Lookin' Good**
   Provide art supplies for the children to make their own poster showing that outward appearances do not make us acceptable to God. Divide the poster into God's side and man's side, with a gulf in between, as shown in the visual under point H of the lesson outline. (This will be similar to the poster provided with the lesson.)

   Discuss:

   Adam and Eve clothed themselves with fig leaves to make themselves acceptable to God. But could their outward appearance make them acceptable to God? (No!)

   What are things people do today to make themselves look good and to try to make themselves acceptable to God? (Doing good deeds; joining the church; giving money to the church.) Do those things make people acceptable to God? (No!)

   On their poster in the section under "man," have the children draw a picture of what Adam and Eve did to make themselves acceptable to God. Then have them draw in that same section what people today try to do to make themselves acceptable to God.

   Reinforce that man is a sinner and is not able to make himself acceptable to God.

Name _____

Greater than all!

Perfect, Holy

ALL-POWERFUL

GOD

IS

Everywhere, all the time

ALL-KNOWING   LOVE   UN-CHANGING

The CREATOR of ALL

 **skit 10** **FIRM FOUNDATIONS**

Adam and Eve Disobeyed God

Readers: Uncle Don, Travis, Jessica

Travis:
Was that ever stupid!

Jessica:
What, Travis?

Travis:
A kid in my class — he got himself expelled from school today.

Uncle Don:
Do you know what happened?

Travis:
Sort of. This kid is always doing dumb stuff. And he steals things sometimes. This time he got caught stealing a tape recorder from the principal's office. Now that is stupid!

Jessica:
Will he have to go to jail?

Travis:
I don't know. I just know he was stupid to do something like that. Anybody would know that's wrong and you can get in big trouble for doing it. He said, "The devil made me do it."

Jessica:
That's **really** stupid! Who would want to follow the devil?

Travis:
Not me!

Jessica:
Me neither!

Uncle Don:
Would you be surprised if I told you that most people who follow the devil didn't really plan to?

Travis:
What do you mean?

Uncle Don:
Satan is very clever. He is totally evil. But he usually disguises himself so that people don't even recognize him.

Jessica:
But isn't everything about him bad?

Uncle Don:
Yes, it is, but he often makes himself appear very good so people are fooled.

Travis:
I don't think he'd fool me.

Uncle Don:
You'd better not speak so quickly, Travis. Satan's very name means deceiver, or tricker.

Jessica:
You mean he plays bad tricks?

Uncle Don:
He certainly does. I want you kids to know what God says about Satan in the Bible. We're going to study Genesis 3 which tells how Satan came to Adam and Eve.

Travis:
You mean he came into the garden?

Uncle Don:
Yes, Travis, he did.

Travis:
I got a book from the library and it says that the story in the Bible about Adam and Eve is just a myth.

Uncle Don:
Travis, that book you got at the library is a very good example of how Satan works to trick or deceive people.

Travis:
But this is a nice book. It has lots of good stuff in it.

Uncle Don:
It may appear that way. But what is written in it is really saying that God is a liar.

Jessica:
A liar! God doesn't lie!

Uncle Don:
No, He doesn't. But this book is saying that the story of Adam and Eve is not really true — it is just a myth. God tells us in many places in His Word that the story of Adam and Eve is true. Who do you suppose is right? God or that library book?

Travis:
I didn't realize, Uncle Don! I was almost tricked into believing that library book just because it looked so good.

Uncle Don:
Travis, there's another danger here. The boy at school said that the devil "made" him do it. I think the story in Genesis 3 will make you think about that statement. People not only are tricked into disobeying God; they also **willfully disobey** Him.

Jessica:
You mean, they do bad things because they want to?

Uncle Don:
I'm afraid so. That's what happened to Adam. 📖

lesson
11
God's Promise and Curse

OVERVIEW

This lesson presents the events that took place immediately following Adam and Eve's sin.

Here in this passage is the first promise of God's plan to send a Deliverer.

Considered in this lesson:

— God's omniscience —
He saw Adam and Eve.

— God's love —
He called Adam.

— God's holiness —
He cursed the serpent, Adam and Eve, and the ground.

— Man's sin —
All men are descendant of Adam; therefore, all sin.

— God's grace —
He promised to send a Deliverer.

LESSON PREPARATION

This section is for you, the teacher.

The passages in the Scripture Reference column are for your own study in preparing for this lesson. Since they may contain concepts that run ahead of the lesson, they are not to be taught at this point.

Note: If you have not taught previously from this series of lessons, please read carefully the note to teachers in the front of this book.

Romans
5:12-21
8:20-22

I Corinthians
15:21, 22

SCRIPTURE: Genesis 3:9-20

LESSON GOALS:

- To show that God knows everything and will punish all sin.
- To show that God would not allow Satan to have a permanent victory in leading man to sin, but that God would send a Deliverer who would overcome Satan and deliver mankind from Satan's power.
- To show the horrible, lasting results of sin.
- To show that man cannot save himself from sin.

THIS LESSON SHOULD HELP THE STUDENTS:

- To realize that no one can get away with sin.
- To realize that God has made a way to overcome Satan.
- To realize that all the problems in the world have come as a result of sin.

PERSPECTIVE FOR THE TEACHER:

You might say that this lesson explains the "mess we are in." We often hear men and women blaming God for their problems and for the problems of the world around them. But Genesis 3 states the truth of the matter very clearly: man's own sin is the cause of man's problems. Children need to know this truth.

Remember that sinners do have reason to fear God's wrath, so in your teaching do not diminish the awful consequences of sin. The introduction of God's grace and His promise to send a Deliverer will be meaningful only if you have clearly taught: (1) man's original position of friendship with his loving Creator and owner, God, (2) the awfulness of man's rebellion and disobedience to God, and (3) the horrible and sure consequences of that sin.

Many people in our society feel that they deserve forgiveness. It is common for children to learn this idea very early in life. But God is holy and righteous and has decreed that the punishment for sin is death. His provision of a Saviour is the supreme act of His grace — totally unmerited favor.

MEMORY
VERSE
Proverbs 9:10

VISUALS:

- Visual showing that Adam and all of Adam's descendants would die
- Poster 5, "Deliverer"; Poster 6, "Mercy"; and Poster 7, "Grace"
- Poster 1, "Learning About God" — Use this to emphasize themes.

SPECIAL PREPARATION:

- Make copies for your class of the **Lesson 11 Review Sheet** and **Skit 11** (at the end of this lesson). Provide pencils for the children.
- Photocopy **visual** (at end of lesson) — use as small poster or for overhead transparency.
- Prepare for any activity you select from the **Suggestions for Activities** (at the end of this lesson). As you select activities, remember to allow sufficient time to teach the outlined lesson material.

ON TEACHING THIS LESSON:

You are carefully laying a scriptural foundation on which the Gospel will later be presented. Each lesson builds on previous lessons, so be sure to cover each point carefully.

DON'T COMPLICATE THE MESSAGE!

As you teach, keep in mind that this is a directed study — not an exhaustive survey of the Bible. Keep your lesson on track and moving ahead by limiting and directing any discussion.

Carefully follow the outline. Emphasize the doctrinal themes.

LESSON FORMAT: The **center column** below contains the lesson material to be taught to the students. The **bold outline headings** are only for reference and need not be spoken, as they are incorporated into the outlined material that follows. The material in the **side columns** is for the teacher's own reference and is not intended to be included in the lesson.

TO BE TAUGHT TO THE STUDENTS
(Center Column Only)

LESSON OUTLINE:

REVIEW Lesson 10, using Lesson 11 Review Sheet.

PERFORM Skit 11. Note: "Uncle Don's" part should be read by an adult.

A. Introduction

Let's listen carefully as we study God's response to Adam and Eve's sin.

Keep in mind:

— God had created them — in His own image and for His glory.

— They belonged to Him.

— He loved them.

— He had given them everything they could ever need.

— He had warned them of the consequences of disobedience.

— They had chosen to disobey Him.

B. God called Adam.

 Theme: God communicates with man.

 READ Genesis 3:9.

Because Adam and Eve didn't come to talk with God, God called out, "Adam, where are you?"

— Why did God call out?

> Didn't He know where they were hiding?
> Isn't He everywhere?
> Wasn't He there beside them among the trees?
> Couldn't He see them all of the time?

— Yes, God could see Adam and Eve where they were hiding.

— Why then did He call Adam?

> God called Adam because, although God intended to punish Adam and Eve for their sin, He still **loved** them.
>
> God was giving them the opportunity **to agree with Him that they were wrong** in believing Satan instead of Him.

God has not changed; He still calls today even though we cannot hear His voice like Adam did.

— How does God call to us today?

> God calls us through all the things we can see around us.
>
> — *Illustrate:*
> *Every day, God's voice is saying to us, "Listen to Me. I am the Creator of all things. I am the true God. I know everything. I am almighty. Look at all the things I have created for you. I love you. Look at all of the food I have made for you. I love you. Look at the life I have given to you. I love you. Listen to Me and seek Me."*

— Every time we see the things God has created, He wants us to think of Him.

— But God is not only speaking to us through the things He has made; He is also calling us through His Word.

— The Bible is God's message to each one of us.

God really wants each one of us to know Him!

C. Adam and Eve tried to hide from God.

 Theme: God knows everything.

 READ Genesis 3:10.

Adam and Eve were afraid of God because they had disobeyed Him.

— Compare:

> *Have you ever hidden when you did something wrong? Why did you hide? You hid because you were ashamed and because you were afraid that you would be punished! Adam and Eve were ashamed, and they were afraid too.*

Adam and Eve had reason to be afraid.

— They knew what they had done.

— And they knew what God had told them would happen if they disobeyed Him.

D. God questioned Adam.

 READ Genesis 3:11.

God questioned Adam and Eve in order to give them an opportunity to repent, that is, to change their minds and agree with God that they had done the wrong thing.

— God had the right to question Adam because He created him.

God created Adam and then made Eve from Adam's rib.

They both belonged to God.

He created them to love and obey Him.

— God also gives life to us and all people.

— Acts 17:25 says, *"...he giveth to all life, and breath...."*

He is our rightful owner.

Adam and Eve had to answer to God for what they did, and we, too, will all have to answer to Him for everything we have thought and done during our lives.

 READ Hebrews 4:13.

God sees everything.

He knows everything we have done.

E. Adam and Eve tried to pass the blame.

 Theme: Man is a sinner. He needs God and is helpless to save himself.

 Theme: God is holy and righteous. He demands death as the payment for sin.

 READ Genesis 3:12,13.

Adam put the blame on Eve.

Eve blamed the serpent.

But God already knew everything that had happened; nothing is hidden from Him.

— Compare:

Have you ever blamed someone else for something you did wrong? Have you ever been blamed for something that someone else did?

We may try to pass the blame onto someone else, as Adam and Eve tried to do; but God knows everything and will not allow anyone to escape punishment by blaming someone else.

F. God's curse on the serpent

 Theme: God is holy and righteous. He demands death as the payment for sin.

 READ Genesis 3:14.

God cursed the serpent because it had been used by Satan.

— God does not tell us what the serpent was like before Satan used it to deceive Eve, but we know it did not slide on its belly when God first created it.

— But now God said it must slide on its belly and eat dust.

God knew it was Satan who spoke through the serpent to tempt Eve.

— God knows everything that Satan and his evil spirits think and plan to do.

— They can't hide anything from God.

God will punish Satan and all of his followers for all of their evil deeds and their horrible disobedience to God.

G. The promised Seed of the woman

Once Adam and Eve disobeyed God and followed the advice of Satan, they were separated from God and controlled by Satan.

Ephesians 2:1, 2

— They were no longer the children of God.

— They were Satan's children.

Satan had become the god of this world.

John 12:31

II Corinthians 4:4

— At this point, Satan probably thought that he had beaten God and that he would now have complete control of the world and all people.

— This was what Satan had wanted.

But no one can win against God.

— God is the almighty Creator.

God promised that He would send a Deliverer who would overcome Satan and deliver mankind from his power. **2**

— Do you know what a Deliverer is?

SHOW POSTER, "DELIVERER." [Read the definition several times and have the children say it until they are understanding what the word means.]

— A deliverer is someone who rescues us or saves us — a deliverer sets us free.

 READ Genesis 3:15.

Isaiah 7:14

Luke 1:27

— God planned that the promised Deliverer would be the child of a virgin woman.

A virgin is a woman who has never married or lived as the wife of a man.

Notice that it does not say "their" offspring.

The man is not even mentioned in this verse.

— When we read of crushing the "head," this is a picture of crushing the leadership or authority of a great power.

When the "head" is crushed, the body cannot survive.

But the one whose "heel" is crushed survives, even though he has been wounded.

— Explain:
The Deliverer would fight against Satan, and the Deliverer would win. Satan would fight against the Deliverer and wound Him, but Satan would not be able to win over Him. This promised Deliverer would destroy Satan and deliver mankind from Satan's power so man would again be in oneness with God.

🔑 **Theme: God is loving, merciful, and gracious.**

2 The introduction of the Deliverer opens up the possibility of many comments from your students. They may ask if Jesus is the Deliverer, to which the reply is, "Yes!"

Let them know that you are eager to talk about Jesus Christ, too, and that you will be glad to talk with any who are interested after class. For right now, though, you will just go on with the story from Genesis. ❏

By studying Genesis 1 and 2, we have already learned many things about God!

READ DOWN THE ENTIRE POSTER, "LEARNING ABOUT GOD" — EXCEPT, READ ONLY, "God is loving...." Leave the rest of this attribute for the next statement:

— Now we also see that God is gracious and merciful.

 READ Psalm 145:8.

Grace and mercy are two wonderful words.

SHOW POSTERS, "GRACE," AND "MERCY."

— "Grace" is God's kindness to undeserving sinners.

— "Mercy" is God's way for sinners to escape the punishment they deserve!

— Explain:

We know from what we have learned about God that He always punishes sin. But in His great love, God promised to make a special way out by sending a Deliverer so that man could be saved from the punishment he deserved.

He could have just left Adam and Eve to die and go to everlasting punishment. That is what they deserved. But God promised a Savior who would deliver them and all mankind from Satan's control and bring them back to God.

H. God's curse on the woman

 READ Genesis 3:16.

God spoke to Eve and told her that because she had disobeyed Him:

— She and all future mothers would suffer in childbirth.

— Her husband would have authority over her.

I. God's curse on the man and on the earth

 READ Genesis 3:17-19.

Adam had foolishly listened to Eve instead of obeying what God had said to him.

— Adam knew what God had said.

— But he was willing to follow Eve's suggestion rather than to do what he knew to be God's will.

Because Adam and Eve listened to Satan, they fell into his trap and disobeyed God.

Therefore, God said that from that time the ground would be cursed.

— Compare:

Before Adam sinned, everything grew without Adam doing any hard work. Weeds didn't grow; there were no pests.

But when Adam sinned, God cursed the earth. Many weeds began to grow. This made Adam's work difficult.

The results of sin affected not only Adam and Eve but also the lovely garden God had given them.

In fact, **all of the bad things in the world exist because of disobedience to God.**

— Satan and his followers disobeyed God and now roam the earth.

— When man disobeyed, his sin affected all of God's creation.

Why should man's sin have affected all creation?

— God had made the earth for man.

— Because He loved man, God gave man everything he needed.

— He wanted man to live in friendship with Him forever.

But now man had disobeyed God.

— Man had rejected God's love for him.

— Part of the consequence was that man would no longer live in a perfect world.

We live in a world that still suffers from that curse.

— People constantly struggle against sickness, pain, weakness, pain in childbearing, hard work, difficult weather conditions, animal and insect pests, weeds, sorrow, grief, and death.

When He created Adam and Eve, God did not intend for them to die.

— But now Adam and Eve must die because of their disobedience to God.

— The punishment for sin is death.

Adam's body must die, just as God had said.

— God had made Adam from the dust of the ground.

— Because Adam sinned, God told Adam that his body must die and go back again to the earth.

J. Adam and Eve are the parents of all people.

 READ Genesis 3:20.

Even though people have different colors of skin, we all originally came from the same parents, Adam and Eve. **3**

Acts 17:26 says that God *"made of one blood all nations of men."*

— Eve is the first woman and the mother of every human being.

— Adam is the father of us all.

Adam was separated from God because he turned away from obeying Him.

— Adam's sin ruined his perfect relationship with God and also the perfection of the earth that God had given him to live in.

— His sin set off a chain of sorrows.

Because of Adam's sin, he would die, and all of his children would also die.

Suggested Graphic:

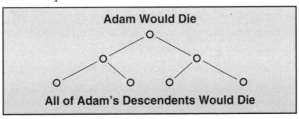

3 This point is very important — don't skip over it. ❏

Isaiah 45:18

Romans 5:12 says that, *"...by one man sin entered into the world, and death by sin; and so death passed upon all men...."*

All people in every country die because we are all the descendants of Adam.

K. Conclusion

The devil did not "make them do it."

— Adam and Eve knew what God had said.
— And they knew that God loved them.
— But they disobeyed Him anyway.

Sin brought terrible consequences.

— We live with those consequences every day.
— In the Bible we have seen how all the sorrows of life began.
— But God, in the very beginning, promised to send a Deliverer — someone to rescue man from Satan, sin and death.

QUESTIONS:

---

1. Did God call Adam because God didn't know where Adam and Eve were? *No, God knew where they were. God wanted them to voluntarily come to Him and admit their sin.*

2. Can anyone hide from God? *No, God sees us at all times, no matter where we are.*

3. Why did God have the right to call Adam and question him?
   a. God was Adam's Creator.
   b. Adam and Eve belonged to God.

4. Why does God have the right to demand obedience? *Because He gave life to everyone.*

5. What was God's curse on the snake? *From that time, it was to move by crawling on its belly.*

6. Whom did God promise to send? *God promised to send a Deliverer.*

7. How was this Deliverer to come? *Through the seed of the woman.*

8. What did God say that the virgin's Son would do? *He would overcome Satan and deliver man from death and Satan's power.*

9. Why did God promise to send a Deliverer? *Because God loves all people.*

10. Did Adam and Eve deserve God's love and His promise of a Deliverer? *No, they deserved to go to everlasting punishment.*

11. What evidence is there in the world today of God's curse on Adam and Eve and on the ground? *Sickness, sorrow, birth pains, death, hard work, thorns and weeds, droughts, devastating storms, poisonous plants, animal and insect pests. These are all signs of God's curse.*

12. Who were the first parents of all people? *Adam and Eve.*

13. Why do all people die? *Because Adam disobeyed God, all Adam's descendants die.*

LESSON 11 — Suggestions for Activities

Be sure to allow time to teach the lesson first!

Listed below are carefully designed activities which will help reinforce and focus on the themes you have taught in the lesson. Choose from this list whatever best suits your students and prepare ahead accordingly. The children may participate in these activities during the time remaining after the lesson has been taught.

1. **Memory Verse — Proverbs 9:10**
   Encourage the children to memorize this verse. Point out: This is what God says about wisdom.

2. **Who's Calling You?**
   Draw the children's attention to things they commonly see and hear that are God's call to people today.

   You could do this activity in several ways. You could take a field trip outside your classroom, or you could bring items to your classroom.

   As you point out each item (bird, tree, sky, kitten, person, flower, the Bible, a book in a library about the Bible, etc.), ask questions such as:

   Where did this flower come from? Who created the original flower from which the seed came for this flower? How is this flower God's call to us? (When we see flowers, we are reminded that God is the Creator, that God is powerful, that God is a God of order, etc. Seeing what God has created helps us know what God is like.)

   Who remembers how we got the Bible? Who is the author of the Bible? Why did God give us the Bible? How is the Bible God's call to us? (The Bible is God's message to us. In it, we learn about Him.)

   Reinforce that God communicates with man.

3. **Why Did They Hide?**
   Write out several typical children's scenarios (samples below) which will help to illustrate why Adam and Eve tried to hide from God. Pass the scenarios out to the children. Have each child read his aloud and answer the question.

   Sample scenarios:

   Tommy broke his mom's favorite vase and hid the pieces. Why did he hide the pieces?

   Ginger and Marie played across the road in a place where they weren't supposed to go. When their parents asked them what they'd been doing, they lied. Why did they hide the truth?

   Discuss:

   Why do people try to hide when they do wrong?

   Why did Adam and Eve hide? Did they have a reason to be afraid?

Reinforce that man is a sinner and that God demands death as the punishment for sin.

Discuss:

Did God know what Adam and Eve had done? Could anyone hide from God?

Reinforce that God knows everything.

4. **Mercy and Grace**
   Before class, prepare handout sheets with the words MERCY and GRACE. Use some sort of fancy lettering which the children can decorate or color. Lettering could be calligraphy or just block letters. Have the children decorate or color their sheets as you discuss God's mercy and grace.

   Discuss:

   Had Adam and Eve sinned? What punishment did they deserve for their sin?

   God made a special promise to Adam and Eve. Do you remember that special promise? (That He would send a Deliverer to save them from the punishment they deserved.) Did Adam and Eve deserve God's love and His promise of a Deliverer? (No, they deserved to go to everlasting punishment.)

   God's promise to Adam and Eve shows His MERCY and His GRACE. What is GRACE? (God's kindness to undeserving sinners.) What is MERCY? (God's way for sinners to escape the punishment they deserve.)

   Reinforce that God is loving, merciful, and gracious.

5. **Consequences**
   Provide supplies for the children to make posters showing how Adam's sin has affected all creation. The children could draw pictures or make a collage using pictures from magazines.

   Discuss:

   Do you remember what God said would happen if Adam and Eve ate from the tree of knowledge of good and evil? (They would die!)

   Today we have also learned that there were other consequences as well. Let's make posters showing how our world today still suffers from the curse. (Remind them that people constantly struggle against sickness, pain, weakness, pain in childbearing, hard work, difficult weather conditions, animal and insect pests, weeds, sorrow, grief, and death.)

   Reinforce that the penalty for sin is death. Because of Adam's sin, he would die, and all of his descendants would die.

Name _____

Adam and Eve Disobeyed God

1. When Satan came to deceive Eve, did he let her know who was talking to her?   YES   NO

2. God told Adam that, if they ate the fruit from the tree of knowledge of good and evil, they would surely die. But Satan told Eve they would not. What was Satan suggesting God to be? _____ _____.

3. Does Satan still try to trick us today?   YES   NO

4. God said that Adam and Eve would die if they ate of the fruit of the tree of the knowledge of good and evil. Satan said they would not die. Who spoke the truth? _____

5. Adam and Eve did not fall dead immediately when they ate of the fruit of the tree of the knowledge of good and evil. God had said that they would die for their disobedience. He meant that:

   They would be _____ from God, their friend and source of life.

   Their _____ would eventually die.

   They would eventually be separated from God forever in the _____ _____ _____.

6. When Adam and Eve realized they were naked, they made clothes of fig leaves for themselves.

   They should have asked _____ for help instead.

7. What did Adam and Eve do when they heard God coming to see them? They _____.

Use this WORD BANK to fill in the answers to the questions above:
bodies   God   a liar   Lake of Fire   hid   God   separated

Knowing God: God is always true. He loves us.

Knowing the Enemy: Satan is a liar and a deceiver. He hates God and man.

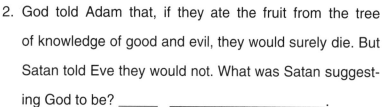

skit 11 God's Promise and Curse

Readers: Uncle Don, Travis, Jessica

Jessica:
Did you hear what happened to Travis yesterday?

Travis:
Jessica!

Uncle Don:
It's all right, Travis, your mom called me and told me about it. How is your hand?

Travis:
It hurts — a lot.

Uncle Don:
You are really bandaged up! I don't think you'll forget that experience for as long as you live.

Travis:
I'd like to.

Uncle Don:
Yes, I imagine you would. I'm glad your dad was there to help you. I thought he wasn't coming back until today. He must have surprised you.

Jessica:
Their meetings were over a day early and he flew back yesterday afternoon.

Travis:
It was awful. I had just turned on the saw. I was going to make a neat present for Dad. Then Jessica hollered at me and scared me. It was her fault!

Jessica:
Travis! It was **your** fault! You disobeyed Dad!

Travis:
I don't think the saw is made right. You shouldn't be able to cut yourself on it.

Uncle Don:
Are you sure it wasn't **my** fault?

Travis:
What do you mean? Oh, I guess I **am** blaming everyone else. It **was** my fault. Anyway, when Jessica hollered, I bumped the saw blade with my hand. It was awful! Somehow, I got the saw turned off. And just then Dad drove up.

Uncle Don:
What did you do, Travis?

Travis:
I didn't know what to do. I tried to hide, but I was bleeding too much. Dad just wrapped a towel around my hand and took me right to the hospital. It was scary.

Jessica:
Mom and I were scared, too. We had to wait so long for Dad to call from the hospital to tell us you were okay!

Uncle Don:
What did the doctor tell you?

Travis:
Well, he said it was really bad. He said I nearly lost the use of my thumb, and I may always have problems with it.

Uncle Don:
Travis, do you realize what happened?

Travis:
What do you mean?

Uncle Don:
Do you realize that your disobedience nearly cost you part of the use of your hand?

Jessica:
It could have killed him.

Uncle Don:
Yes, if someone hadn't been there to help you, you could have bled to death. Travis, I hate to see that you've been hurt so badly, but maybe it will help you see the seriousness of sin. That's just what we're going to study about in Genesis. There are consequences to sin, and I'm afraid you are facing some of them.

Jessica:
That's what Dad told him when they got home.

Travis:
You know something? I was so afraid that Dad was going to be mad at me. But he didn't say hardly anything on the way to the hospital. He just kept looking over at me and asking me if I was doing all right.

Uncle Don:
Your Dad loves you, Travis.

Travis:
I know. He promised to teach me to use the saw one day, when I get older. He did bawl me out when we got home, but he did something I've never seen him do. He and mom cried.

Jessica:
We all cried.

Uncle Don:
Travis, sin affects everyone. We're going to read about Adam and Eve, and I want you to see how they acted and how God responded to their sin. I think that you will identify a little with what happened. And God made a promise too — a wonderful promise for sinners. 📖

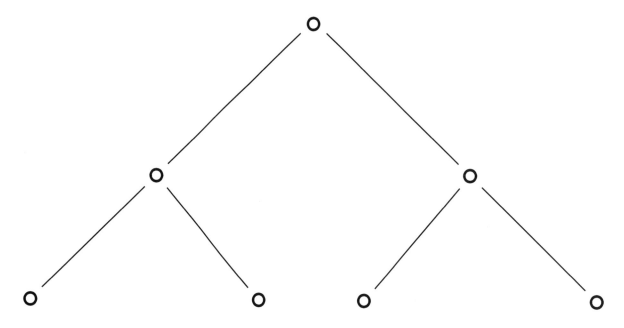

Adam Would Die

All of Adam's Descendants Would Die

lesson 12

God's Provision and Judgment; The Birth of Cain and Abel

OVERVIEW

This passage of Scripture emphasizes God's holiness and His grace. Here we see the first blood sacrifice for sin and God's gracious act of clothing Adam and Eve. God is establishing the fact of man's helplessness to save himself and providing an analogy regarding the coming Deliverer.

Some points:

— The clothing Adam and Eve had made for themselves was not acceptable to God.

— God made clothing of skins for them.

— God put Adam and Eve out of the garden and guarded the entrance so they could never return.

— God is the giver of all life.

— Cain and Abel were born outside of the garden; they were born sinners.

— All of Adam's descendents were and are born sinners, separated from God

LESSON PREPARATION
This section is for you, the teacher.

The passages in the Scripture Reference column are for your own study in preparing for this lesson. Since they may contain concepts that run ahead of the lesson, they are not to be taught at this point.

Note: If you have not taught previously from this series of lessons, please read carefully the note to teachers in the front of this book.

SCRIPTURE: Genesis 3:21-24; 4:1, 2

LESSON GOALS:

- To show that God knows everything and will punish all sin.

- To show that man cannot save himself from sin.

- To show that only God can make man acceptable in His sight.

- To show that the sin of Adam has been passed on to all men.

THIS LESSON SHOULD HELP THE STUDENTS:

- To realize that they are sinners.

- To realize that no one can "get away with" sin.

- To realize that there is nothing they can do to make themselves acceptable to God.

PERSPECTIVE FOR THE TEACHER:

This lesson introduces some basic principles that much of our society has chosen to blur or even totally reject. Sadly, among those who reject these truths are many so-called Christian groups who have chosen, as Paul said, *"another gospel"* (Galatians 1:6).

First of all, the Word is very clear in stating that God killed animals in order to make acceptable coverings for Adam and Eve. Although the blood of animals could never pay for sin, from this time until the death of Christ, God accepted the blood of animals as a type, or picture, of the punishment that all sin deserves. Romans 6:23 says, *"For the wages of sin is death...."* Hebrews 9:22 says, *"...without shedding of blood is no remission."*

Secondly, the Word shows us that man cannot come to God on man's terms; man must come to God in the way that God has provided as His acceptable way. Adam and Eve's clothing of leaves was not acceptable to God; neither is anything that we might do to try to make ourselves acceptable to God.

Refusal or distortion of these two principles has given rise to many false religions. How tempted man is to follow a religion that overlooks the heavy penalty for sin! How tempted man is to try to find his own way to take care of his sin problem! How deceitful sin is! How deceitful man's heart is! And how deceitful the Enemy is!

If Satan can get us to "feel religious" and still miss the truth of God's Word, he has subtly cut us off from God and from eternal life. As long as a man feels adequately religious, he is not going to seek to know more about God. John 9:41

MEMORY
VERSE
Hebrews 4:13

records Jesus' words to the Pharisees: *"...If ye were blind, ye should have no sin: but now ye say, We see; therefore your sin remaineth."*

This is the story of the first blood sacrifice for sin, and it shows us that God will accept only those who come to Him in the way He prescribes.

Many religious groups would call this teaching "narrow." Jesus did, too! Matthew 7:13,14 quotes His words: *"Enter ye in at the strait [narrow] gate: for wide is the gate, and broad is the way, that leadeth to destruction, and many there be which go in thereat: Because strait [narrow] is the gate, and narrow is the way, which leadeth unto life, and few there be that find it."*

May we be faithful to help the children to see and to choose the narrow way! The truths in this lesson are an essential part of the foundation upon which the rest of the truths of that narrow way can be firmly established.

VISUALS:

- Chronological Picture No. 6, "Fig Leaf Coverings"

- Chronological Picture No. 7, "Adam and Eve Driven from the Garden"

- Chronological Chart

- Poster 1, "Learning About God" — Use this to emphasize themes.

- Poster 8, "Adam and all his descendants are sinners"

- Poster 4, "God and Man"

- Visual "Separation between Adam and all of Adam's descendants, and God"

SPECIAL PREPARATION:

- Make copies for your class of the **Lesson 12 Review Sheet** and **Skit 12** (at the end of this lesson). Provide pencils for the children.

- Photocopy **visual** (at end of lesson) — use as small poster or for overhead transparency.

- Prepare for any activity you select from the **Suggestions for Activities** (at the end of this lesson). As you select activities, remember to allow sufficient time to teach the outlined lesson material.

ON TEACHING THIS LESSON:

You are carefully laying a scriptural foundation on which the Gospel will later be presented. Each lesson builds on previous lessons, so be sure to cover each point carefully.

DON'T COMPLICATE THE MESSAGE!

As you teach, keep in mind that this is a directed study — not an exhaustive survey of the Bible. Keep your lesson on track and moving ahead by limiting and directing any discussion.

Carefully follow the outline. Emphasize the doctrinal themes.

LESSON FORMAT: The **center column** below contains the lesson material to be taught to the students. The **bold outline headings** are only for reference and need not be spoken, as they are incorporated into the outlined material that follows. The material in the **side columns** is for the teacher's own reference and is not intended to be included in the lesson.

TO BE TAUGHT TO THE STUDENTS
(Center Column Only)

LESSON OUTLINE:

REVIEW Lesson 11, using Lesson 12 Review Sheet.

PERFORM Skit 12. Note: "Uncle Don's" part should be read by an adult.

A. Introduction

Do you want to understand why things happen as they do in this world?

Study the Bible!

The things recorded in Genesis 3 affected **all** mankind — every person who has ever lived — including you and me.

God cares about us and wants us to know Him.

So let's open our Bibles again and continue to study Genesis 3.

B. God refused the clothing which Adam and Eve had made.

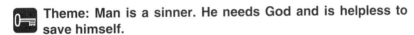 **Theme: Man is a sinner. He needs God and is helpless to save himself.**

 **Theme: Man can come to God only according to God's will and plan.**

 READ Genesis 3:21.

Let's read again what Adam and Eve had done to try to cover their nakedness.

 READ Genesis 3:7.

Suggested Visual:

CHRONOLOGICAL PICTURE NO. 6. "FIG LEAF COVERINGS."

— They made themselves coverings of leaves.

— Because they had disobeyed God, they were embarrassed to have God see them naked.

But God refused to accept the clothes which Adam and Eve had made.

— Why?

Isaiah 64:6

Ephesians 2:8, 9

He wanted to teach them that they couldn't do **anything** to make themselves acceptable to God.

God will not accept anything that is done according to man's ideas.

God only accepts whatever is done according to His way.

No one can do anything to make himself acceptable to God.

POINT TO POSTER, "GOD AND MAN."

People today still do many things to try to make themselves acceptable to God; they try to "cover" for their sins, just as Adam and Eve did.

— Example:

Some people think that if they go to church or do a lot of good deeds, it will help to make up for the wrongs they have done.

You can probably think of lots of other examples of this kind of "do-it-yourself" covering for sin. God sees right through it, and it is completely unacceptable to Him.

C. God killed animals.

 Theme: God is holy and righteous. He demands death as the payment for sin.

The first death in the world was brought about by sin.

— God killed animals.

　　The animals' blood was shed.

　　God then took the skins off the animals.

— Adam and Eve did not do this; God killed the animals, and He took the skins off.

— God was reminding Adam and Eve that disobedience to Him brought death into the world. **1**

D. God provided clothing for Adam and Eve.

 Theme: God is loving, merciful, and gracious.

Why did God kill the animals?

To provide clothing for guilty Adam and Eve.

— God provided them with clothing made from the skins of the animals which He had killed.

— God did this for Adam and Eve, even though they did not deserve it.

Only God could supply them with clothing which would make them acceptable to Him.

E. God put coats of skin on Adam and Eve.

God put coats of skin on Adam and Eve.

— He didn't just give them clothing and tell them to put it on.

— God put the clothing, which He made, on Adam and Eve.

1 Here God is preparing a redemptive analogy of the truth presented in Isaiah 61: 10, "...he hath clothed me with the garments of salvation, he hath covered me with the robe of righteousness...." Later, we will draw on this analogy to reveal the truth of substitution and the covering of the righteousness of Christ received through faith. Do not apply this truth to your students yet by telling them the Gospel. Just make it clear that God would not accept what Adam and Eve had made but that God provided them with clothing, and that what we do outwardly cannot make us pleasing to God. This is all you need to say at this point. You are laying foundations and establishing spiritual principles. Later on, when teaching the Gospel, you will point back to this illustration. ❏

F. God put Adam and Eve out of the garden, away from the tree of life.

 Theme: God is holy and righteous. He demands death as the payment for sin.

 READ Genesis 3:22,23.

God the Father, God the Son, and God the Holy Spirit said this.

They were talking about Adam and Eve.

— When God first made Adam and Eve, they didn't know anything evil or bad.

— They only knew what was good.
   Everything God made and gave to them was good.
   Everything God told them to do was good.

— But when they disobeyed God their Creator, they found that not everything was good. **2**

Satan had deceived Eve so she thought the fruit from the tree of the knowledge of good and evil would be good for food.

But as soon as Adam and Eve ate that fruit:

— They were ashamed and afraid.

— Now they knew that not everything was good but that some things were evil.

Adam and Eve should have trusted God.

— God knew what was good and what was evil.

— Adam and Eve should have trusted Him to tell them instead of finding out for themselves.

God had given them every good thing to eat — He had even offered to them the opportunity to eat from the tree of life.

But they had **chosen to disobey God** and to eat, instead, from the tree of the knowledge of good and evil — the one tree from which God had forbidden them to eat.

Now, because they had disobeyed God, **He would not allow them to eat of the tree of life.**

— Consider:

   Genesis 3:22 says that the reason God put them out of the garden was so that they would not eat of the tree of life and live forever.

   This was actually an act of God's mercy.

   God did not want men to physically live forever as sinners. (Can you imagine what the world would be like if all the evil men that ever lived were still alive now?)

Because they were separated from God, they would also have to die physically.

Therefore, God put Adam and Eve, the father and mother of us all, out of the garden, away from the tree of life.

 Theme: God is greater than all and more important than all; He is the highest authority.

2 Someone may ask, "If God created everything perfect, how could anything be bad?" You might remind them that Satan had chosen to disobey God. He became evil. ❑

153

— Compare:

When Satan sinned, God put him out of his wonderful position in Heaven. Now, because of God's hatred for sin, He also put Adam and Eve out of the garden.

God doesn't ask anyone what He should do; He is the supreme One in the whole universe.

— No one can fight against God and win.

— We cannot trick or deceive God.

He hates disobedience to His commands and will not allow any disobedient person to live with Him.

G. God put cherubim and a flaming sword to guard the way to the tree of life.

 Theme: Man is a sinner. He needs God and is helpless to save himself.

 READ Genesis 3:24.

Suggested Visual:

CHRONOLOGICAL PICTURE NO. 7, "ADAM AND EVE DRIVEN FROM THE GARDEN"

At the east of the garden of Eden, God put some of His good angels called cherubim and a sword of fire which turned every way to make sure that Adam and Eve could not return and eat the fruit from the tree of life.

— If they had tried to go back, the good angels of God would have seen them, and Adam and Eve would have been killed by the sword of fire.

— There was nothing they could do. **3**

— When God put them out of the garden, that was the end.

— There was absolutely no way they could get back to the tree of life.

They would now grow old and die.

H. God is the giver of life.

 Theme: God is greater than all and more important than all; He is the highest authority.

 READ Genesis 4:1.

Eve said this because she knew that God is the giver of all life.

— God made Adam from the dust of the ground and breathed into him to give him life.

3 When teaching that man was put out of the garden, we must stress that there was no way back. Through the teaching of God's Word, we are laying the foundations for our students to realize that, if God doesn't make a way back to Him, they are destined for eternal punishment. ❏

Psalm 100:3

Acts 17:25

— God made Eve from Adam's rib.

— Every person is given life by God.

— Your life was given to you by God.

— Psalm 100:3 says, *"Know ye that the LORD he is God: it is he that hath made us, and not we ourselves...."*

CHRONOLOGICAL CHART: Point to the names "Cain and Abel."

I. Cain and Abel were both born outside of the garden.

 Theme: Man is a sinner. He needs God and is helpless to save himself.

 READ Genesis 4:2.

Because Adam and Eve had sinned against God, they were put outside of the garden, away from the tree of life.

— Cain and Abel were born outside of the garden, away from the tree of life, because Adam, their father, was outside of the garden.

— Cain and Abel were born sinners because their father, Adam, was a sinner.

    Had Adam not sinned, Cain and Abel would have been born with the ability to know, love, and obey God.

    Instead, they were born under Satan's control.

Not only was Adam the father of Cain and Abel, but he was also the father of the whole human race.

— Adam was your forefather.

— He was my forefather.

— He was everyone's forefather.

Romans 5:12

Therefore, because Adam disobeyed God and was separated from Him, all people in this world are born sinners, cut off from God and with Satan as their father.

SHOW POSTER, "ADAM — SINNER."

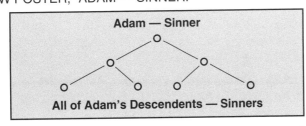

Adam — Sinner

All of Adam's Descendents — Sinners

— Explain:

We do not like to think of being born with a disposition to sin. But think for a moment about the little children you know — do you have a little brother or sister? Do they always obey? Do you always obey? No. Children are not born with a nature to obey; they must be taught. Have you ever heard a baby learn to say yes before he learned to say no? Have you ever seen a little child who wanted to do everything that his parents asked him to do, just when his parents asked him to do it? No.

We are, in many ways, a product of our parents, and of their parents, and of their parents' parents, and so on, all the way back to Adam. We have inherited many things, like the color of our eyes and hair, and we have learned a lot about how to behave from our parents. But we have also inherited the nature to sin. We are the product of sinners; and the line of sin can be traced through every generation right back to Adam, the father of the human race.

God is the One who gives life to all people, but we are not born in friendship or oneness with God.

Suggested Visual:

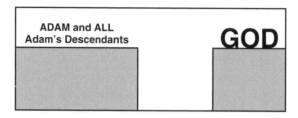

— Satan has taken God's place as our spiritual father.

What does this mean?

It means that we, too, just like Cain and Abel, were born unable to know, love, and obey God.

From birth we are under Satan's control.

— It is important that we realize we were born sinners.

— We were born separated from God, with Satan as our father, just as every other human being is born separated from God.

We must also remember that, even though we are born sinners, it is God who has given us life.

— All life comes from God.

— All life is owned by God.

— He created everyone and everything.

— Contrast:

Some people like to think that we are "all God's children." That sounds good, doesn't it! But that's not what the Bible says.

The Bible tells us that God created us. But Adam's sin put all men into Satan's family. So we are not born "God's children," but Satan's children, cut off from God.

J. Conclusion

What we are reading from the Bible is true history.

— Adam and Eve were real people, and we are their descendants.

— God mentions their story and their names even in the New Testament.

— Adam and Eve's sin affected all of us.

God has written these things for us so we can know Him.

QUESTIONS:

1. Why did God refuse the clothes which Adam and Eve made? *Because God wanted to teach Adam and Eve that they couldn't do anything to make themselves acceptable to God.*

2. Can a person make himself acceptable to God by anything that he does? *No.*

3. What are some of the things you can think of that men do to try to make themselves acceptable to God?

4. Will God accept any of these things? *No.*

5. Who is the only One who could make Adam and Eve acceptable to God? *God.*

6. Why did God kill animals to make clothing for Adam and Eve? *Because God was reminding Adam and Eve that the punishment for sin is death.*

7. Why did God make them clothes? *Because, even though they had sinned, He still loved them, and He wanted to show them that He was the only One who could make them acceptable to Him.*

8. In what way did Adam and Eve become like God after they ate the fruit of the tree of the knowledge of good and evil? *They now knew that there was evil as well as good.*

9. Why did God put Adam and Eve out of the garden of Eden? *So that they wouldn't be able to eat the fruit from the tree of life and live forever in sin.*

10. How did God make sure they wouldn't be able to return? *He placed angels called cherubim and a sword of fire flashing every direction to keep them away.*

11. Can anyone trick or deceive God? *No.*

12. Who gives every person his life? *God.*

13. Where were Cain and Abel born? *Outside of the garden of Eden.*

14. Why were Cain and Abel born sinners and separated from God? *Because of their father, Adam.*

15. Why were we all born sinners and separated from God? *Because Adam is also our father.*

LESSON 12 — Suggestions for Activities

Be sure to allow time to teach the lesson first!

Listed below are carefully designed activities which will help reinforce and focus on the themes you have taught in the lesson. Choose from this list whatever best suits your students and prepare ahead accordingly. The children may participate in these activities during the time remaining after the lesson has been taught.

1. Memory Verse — Hebrews 4:13

As the children learn the verse, reinforce that God sees and knows everything — even our thoughts.

2. Before and After

Provide art supplies for the children to make a poster. Make two columns, as shown below. Have the children draw pictures of Adam and Eve in the garden before they sinned and being driven out of the garden after they sinned (or use copies of Chronological Drawings No. 4 and No. 7.)

Underneath the pictures, have the children write how life was for Adam and Eve in each situation. The finished poster will look something like this:

Before they sinned	After they sinned

friendship with God	separated from God
could eat from the tree of life	could not eat from the tree of life
no fear	fear
no sickness	sickness
no pain	pain
no weeds	weeds
easy work	hard work
rulers over the earth	Satan now god of this world
no death	death
created perfect	all descendants would sin and would die

Discuss:

What did Adam and Eve deserve when they sinned? (Death)

Could Adam and Eve change any of the things caused by their sin? (No. Only God could help them.)

Reinforce the tremendous consequences of sin. We are still living with those consequences.

3. Born Sinners

Provide art supplies for the children to draw copies of the class visuals showing that all of Adam's descendants are born sinners and born separated from God. (See *Suggested Visuals* in the lesson.) (For the visual showing that all are sinners, you may want to suggest that the children draw stick figures instead of little circles to represent Adam's descendants.)

Discuss:

Where were Cain and Abel born? Why were they born outside the garden and away from the tree of life? (Because Adam, their father, was outside of the garden.)

(Point to the appropriate class visuals as you ask...) Why were Cain and Abel born as sinners? Why were they born separated from God? (Because their father Adam was a sinner and separated from God.)

Why were all people born as sinners and separated from God? (Because Adam is the father of all people.)

Let's make copies of these visuals so each of you will have a reminder of this important truth.

Reinforce that man is a sinner.

4. Family Tree

Help the children draw a family tree that shows them, their parents, and their grandparents. (To represent each person, they could use names, pictures, or drawings.)

Discuss:

Does anyone ever say to you, "You're just like your dad," or maybe, "You're just like your mom"? How are you like your dad? How are you like your mom? What physical traits or personality characteristics did you inherit from your parents? (Color of eyes, hair color, skin color, blood type, way of walking, happy-go-lucky personality, etc.)

Did your parents inherit characteristics from their parents? And did your grandparents inherit characteristics from their parents? In many ways, we are a product of our parents and of their parents.

Who is the forefather of all people? Let's write the name "Adam" on our family tree to show that he is our forefather.

Do you remember from our lesson what all people have inherited from Adam? (Point to the class visuals.)

Reinforce that all of Adam's descendants are born sinners and separated from God.

God's Promise and Curse

1. After Adam and Eve had sinned, God called to them because He wanted them to _____ their sin.

2. Can anyone hide from God?   YES   NO

3. God had the right to question Adam because God _____ Adam. Adam belonged to God.

4. God promised to send a Deliverer who would overcome _____ and deliver men from death.

5. God promised to send a Deliverer because God _____ people.

6. Did Adam and Eve deserve God's love and His promise to send a Deliverer?   YES   NO

7. Who were the first parents of all people? _____ and _____

8. All people _____ because Adam, the first man disobeyed God.

Use this WORD BANK to fill in the answers to the questions above:

loves   Adam and Eve   admit   Satan   created   sin

ACREG ___ ___ ___ ___ ___

Unscramble the letters to find the word that means

GOD'S UNDESERVED KINDNESS

VELIDRERE

___ ___ ___ ___ ___ ___ ___ ___ ___

Unscramble the letters to find the word that means

SOMEONE WHO RESCUES, SAVES US

On the back of this paper, write out Hebrews 4:13 and then memorize it.

GOD SEES SIN

MAN'S SIN BROUGHT GOD'S CURSE.

In the beginning, God created everything perfect and good. But when man **sinned**, all of God's creation suffered from the curse.

Pain, sickness, death, hard work, sorrow, separation, fear, destruction, disease, violent weather, all started as the result of man's _____.

  FIRM FOUNDATIONS   REVIEW SHEET

God's Provision and Judgment

Readers: Uncle Don, Travis, Jessica

Uncle Don:
How is your hand doing, Travis?

Travis:
It still hurts a lot. But I think it's a little better.

Jessica:
It would be better if he didn't keep banging it.

Travis:
I know. But it's hard not to. I keep trying to do stuff for myself, but I just can't do it. It's embarrassing. I even need help getting dressed.

Uncle Don:
I can sympathize with you. I hurt my hand real badly once. But it's a good reminder that there are some things we really can't do for ourselves. We need help.

Jessica:
Like what?

Uncle Don:
Well, there are lots of things we need help with, but I was thinking particularly of our sin problem. God won't accept anything we try to do ourselves to take care of our sins.

Jessica:
Doesn't the Bible say, "God helps those who help themselves?"

Uncle Don:
No, that's something man thought of. It's not found anywhere in the Bible.

Travis:
It's hard not to be able to help yourself. I'm tired of it. I can't do anything with this big bandage.

Uncle Don:
We really like to do things ourselves, don't we?

Travis:
Dad said he did something almost like I did when he was just a little boy.

Jessica:
He did? What did he do?

Travis:
Well, he disobeyed his dad, just like I did.

Jessica:
Disobeyed? Dad disobeyed his dad?

Travis:
He did! He was told not to use this big axe they had for chopping firewood.

Jessica:
What happened?

Travis:
He used it anyway. He said he thought he was getting pretty good at splitting wood when he missed and hit his foot.

Jessica:
Oh, how awful!

Travis:
It was awful. He said that's why he limps a little now. I never thought about it before. He showed me the scar. It must have been really bad.

Jessica:
I just can't imagine Dad disobeying!

Travis:
I can!

Uncle Don:
Kids, I think you need to understand something. We are all sinners. We were born sinners.

Jessica:
Born sinners?

Uncle Don:
Yes, born sinners. We have inherited a lot of things from our parents, and they inherited a lot of things from their parents (your grandparents), and so on. We inherit our hair color, our eye color, our height, and lots of other things.

Travis:
But what's that got to do with being born a sinner?

Uncle Don:
Travis, do you remember what we said about everyone being related to Adam?

Travis: .
Adam and Eve were the first parents of all people.

Uncle Don:
That's right. And because Adam sinned, his sin was passed on to his children and to their children and right on down to us. Everyone is born a sinner because we are descendants of Adam who sinned.

Jessica:
That's not fair!

Uncle Don:
Jessica, man rebelled against his Creator. Sin affected **everything** in all creation.

Jessica:
Can't we do something about it?

Uncle Don:
No, there's nothing we can do. Only God can help us.

**ADAM and ALL
of Adam's
Descendants**

GOD

Visuals

On the following pages you will find visuals of Posters 7-16. (Note: There is no Poster 9.) These visuals may be photocopied for classroom use, and are specifically designed to be copied for use on an overhead projector.

The visuals for Posters 1-6 are in the back of Book 1.

Grace

God's kindness to undeserving sinners

FIRM FOUNDATIONS

Adam

SINNER

all Adam's descendants

SINNERS

FIRM FOUNDATIONS

Some of
GOD'S PROMISES
to Abraham

- To make from Abraham a great nation

- To bless all peoples on the earth through Abraham

- To make Abraham's descendants slaves in another country for 400 years, to punish that country, and to bring Abraham's descendants out with great possessions

Through
ISRAEL

- God was going to send the Deliverer

- God gave His Word to the whole world

- God was preserving the true knowledge of Himself

FIRM FOUNDATIONS

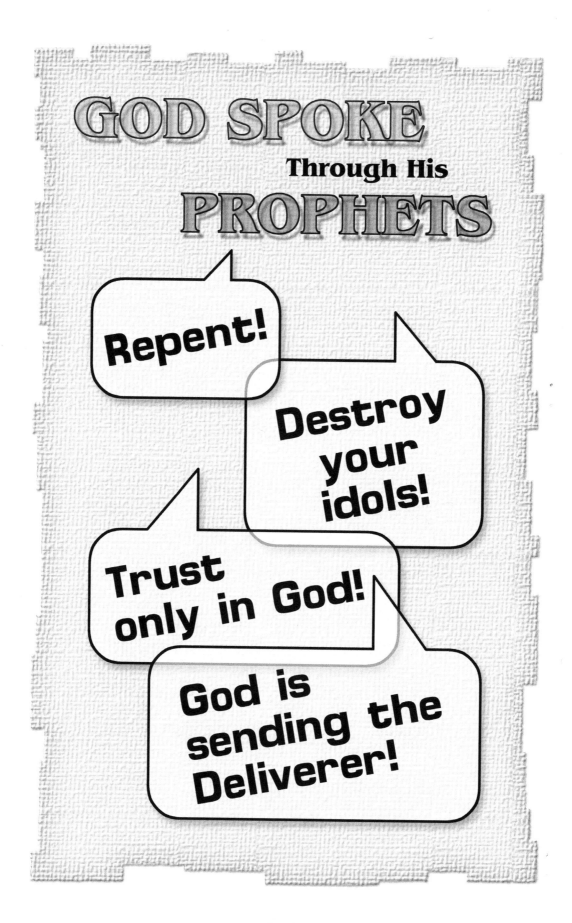

JESUS CHRIST IS GOD

Jesus Christ is man

Jesus Christ is holy and righteous

Jesus Christ is the only Saviour

FIRM FOUNDATIONS

What GOD Said Would Happen To
The Deliverer

Isaiah 9:7	David's descendant
Isaiah 7:14	Born of a virgin
Micah 5:2	Born in Bethlehem
Hosea 11:1	Flee into Egypt
Isaiah 11:2	Some of His characteristics
Isaiah 53:4,5	Suffer for others
Psalm 41:9	Betrayed by a friend
Zec. 11:12,13	Sold for 30 pieces of silver
Psalm 27:12	Accused by false witnesses
Isaiah 50:6	Smitten and spat upon
Isaiah 53:7	Silent when accused
Isaiah 53:3	Rejected by Jews
Psalm 69:4	Hated without a cause
Psalm 22:16	His hands and feet pierced
Psalm 22:18	His clothing gambled for
Isaiah 53:12	Die with the wicked
Psalm 22:6-8	Mocked and insulted
Isaiah 53:9	Buried with the rich
Psalm 16:10	Rise again
Psalm 68:18	Go back to Heaven

©1993, 2001 New Tribes Mission

148-759

  FIRM FOUNDATIONS

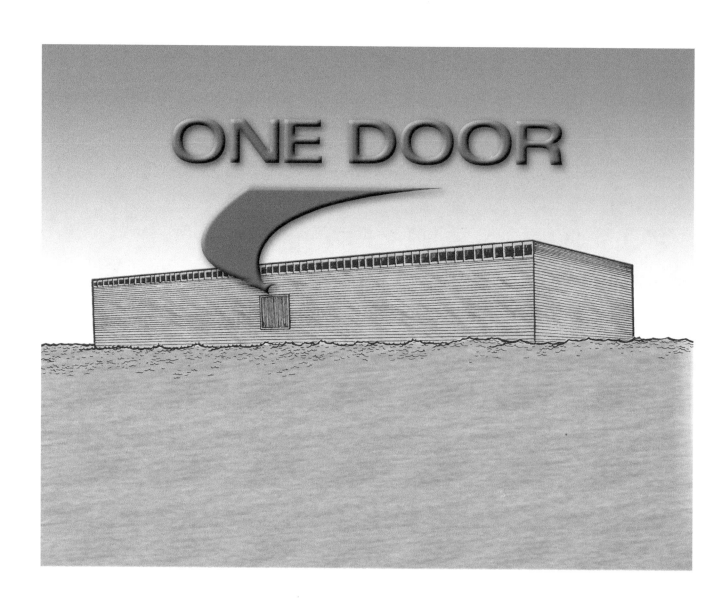

FIRM FOUNDATIONS

© New Tribes Mission, 1993
Permission given to photocopy for classroom use